Indian Citizenship Decoded

Beyond Emotional Outburst and Political Predilections

Sanhita Mukherjee

Copyright © 2021 Sanhita Mukherjee All rights reserved

The characters and events portrayed in this book are fictitious. Any similarity to real persons, living or dead, is coincidental and not intended by the author.

No part of this book may be reproduced, or stored in a retrieval system, or transmitted in any form or by any means, electronic, mechanical, photocopying, recording, or otherwise, without express written permission of the publisher.

ISBN-13: 9798528665788

Cover by Amazon KDP® Cover Creator and Author

Published in August 2021 at Kolkata, West Bengal, India

Foreword

The debates over the Citizenship (Amendment) Act 2019 created huge national clamor. The pandemonium enhanced the confusion. I felt it necessary to know what the Citizenship Act, 1955 was before the amendments of 2019. Yet my laziness found too many ways to carve out the necessary time from my schedule. Then came a push from Mr. Rajarshi Chattopadhyay, Founder-Editor, Nayadashak, a Bangla periodical with a web version, for a write-up on the matter.

I have not yet sent anything to Mr. Chattopadhyay. I could not. The subject seemed too humongous to study quickly. I had to take notes and jot down my observations. When the wordcount crossed ten thousand, I decided to sum up my quest in a book. Hence, this book happened.

I had to roam around complicated phrases of bare acts to arrive at my findings. I am not a lawyer. But I have worked under several laws while working for the Government of West Bengal. To get things done, every now and then, I had to understand those laws in letter and spirit. In those days, I developed my own method of untangling complex legal statements.

I have applied the same method to understand the laws about Indian citizenship. I read them as follows:

Condition A holds if

Condition B is true

Condition C is true

Under circumstance (i)

Under paradigm (a)

Under paradigm (b)

Under circumstance (ii)

Thus, for me any legal statement is a bunch of conditional statements. Untangling the conditions, conditions nested within conditions, I have got to the core of the legal statements.

I have categorized all principal clauses that state a Section of the laws as "Condition A" in the above example. Conditions B and C stood for all subsections of the law. Then circumstances (i), (ii) were mapped to clauses under a section/ sub-section of the law. Finally, paradigm (a), (b) et cetera were mapped to sub-clauses under a clause under a subsection / section of the law. In the constitution, the sections have been replaced with Articles.

This endeavor has made most part of this book a structured breakdown of existing bare acts on the citizenship of India. It has also incorporated the debates over 2019 amendments of the Citizenship Act, 1955.

It can come in handy for the aspirants of examinations for different public services. It can be helpful to those who are in between citizenships of India and other countries and looking forward to obtaining an Overseas Citizen of India Card. It can also be guiding material to those who have somehow lost citizenship of India and seeking a way to acquire it. It can also be a guide to finding one's ancestor in the Legacy Data if Nationwide NRC is ever notified. It can be entertaining to the curious souls who have an urge to understand what citizenship of India is beyond brouhaha in the media.

It is a multipurpose book. It aspires to cater to multitudes of needs and various interests.

None of these could have been possible without relentless support from Partha, my spouse. No word of acknowledgement is enough for his endless patience over my endeavor.

Contents

INTRODUCTION 7

CONSTITUTION OF INDIA ON CITIZENSHIP OF INDIA 10

THE CITIZENSHIP ACT, 1955 AS AMENDED 14

- SECTIONS 1 & 2 14
- SECTION 3 18
- SECTION 4 20
- SECTION 5 23
- SECTION 6 26
- SECTION 6A 30
- SECTION 7 35
- SECTION 7A 36
- SECTION 7B 40
- SECTION 7C 42
- SECTION 7D 43
- SECTION 8 45
- SECTION 9 46
- SECTION 10 47
- SECTIONS 11 AND 12 49
- SECTION 13 51
- SECTION 14 52
- SECTION 14 A 53
- SECTION 15 54
- SECTIONS 15A, 16 55
- SECTION 17, 18 56
- SECTION 19, SUMMARY 60

THE CITIZENSHIP RULES, 2003 62

NRC – PROCESS FOLLOWED IN ASSAM 82

HULLABALOO ABOUT CAA, 2019 97

REFERENCES I

Introduction

This book is an attempt to seek what citizenship is meant in India. The search is strictly confined in statutes. It starts with the leading stone of statutes – the Constitution of India. Then it delves into the Citizenship Act, 1955 as amended till 2015. Finally, it searches through Citizenship (Amendment) Act, 2019, popularly abbreviated as CAA, 2019. Besides, it delves in appraisal if CAA, 2019 is against secular ethos enshrined in the Constitution of India and, also, if the aforementioned amendment stands against the ideal of equality enshrined in the same Constitution. But it does not play statutory authority and passes any verdict on the issues still *sub judice*. Moreover, it narrates the citizenship rules of 2003 for registration of citizens and issue of national identity cards. It also summarizes the provisions of the National Citizen Register held in Assam. However, the goal of the book is to ease up reading of law by simplifying complex constructions of legal codes.

Citizenship of India was first defined in the Part II of the Constitution of India. Guided by the vision of citizenship in India laid by the Constitution came the Citizenship Act, 1955. This act has subsequently been amended in 1985, 1986, 1992, 2004, 2005, 2015 and 2019. The first amendment occurred after thirty years since the first inception of the act. The amendments of 2004 saw a sea change in determining Indian citizenship. Besides, these amendments got rid of certain ambiguities regarding actual human beings and corporations. Some of the sections of these amendments are shortest lived statutes. The span of existence of such laws was as short as six months. Compared to this amendment, the latest amendment of 2019 is quite smaller.

There are sections in the Citizenship Act, 1955, as amended up to date, which have never been amended since the inception in 1955. Such sections are 10 and 13. Also, subsection (1) under Section 9 has never been amended. This appears exceptional among several amendments on a single section, often in a frenzied manner over subsequent years, as if public opinion regarding matters of those sections were shifted within six months.

The quest for definition of citizen of India has gained huge momentum after recent amendments to the Citizenship Act, 1955. Considering this fact, this book has emphasized to mention different changes occurred during different amendments. Though it is the norm to mention amended laws with the amended word in parenthesis, e.g., the Citizenship (Amendment) Act, 2004 and the Citizenship (Amendment) Act, 2019, yet giving in to popular discourse, this book chose to mention all the amendment acts regarding the Citizenship Act, 1955 as "CAA" followed by the year of amendment.

Through subsequent chapters the book has discussed the provisions of citizenship of India in the Constitution of India and through different sections of the Citizenship Act, 1955 as amended. These chapters are designed more towards emanating exact information in the statute than flaring controversies.

Under the current environment, the National Register of Citizens has become a household matter. Keeping an eye on the pertinence of National Register of Citizens, popularly known as NRC, this book has included a chapter on the Citizenship (Registration of Citizens and Issue of National Identity Card) Rules, 2003. This chapter is a summary of untangled statements of the aforesaid rule.

There was a huge hue and cry over the recently concluded National Register of Citizens procedures in Assam. This book has described the forms and processes followed in NRC conducted in Assam. Thus, it has summarized the documents required by the citizens to establish their proof of citizenship.

This book has a concluding chapter regarding the debates on CAA, 2019. This chapter has mainly summarized the constitutional provisions, scholarly articles, reports by the government agencies of different countries and the United Nations and media publications to cover the gamut of the issue in its entirety. It has resorted to historic statements of the Supreme Court in finding the resolution over the debate.

Constitution of India on Citizenship of India

In the Constitution of India, citizenship is defined in Part II. The articles that define citizenship are Article 5, Article 6, and Article 8. Article 7 and Article 9 lay out the factors that exclude persons from being citizens of India. Article 10 spells out how citizenship of India can be continued. Article 11 vests power in the Parliament for making laws regarding citizenship in India.

Article 5 defines citizenship by –

i. birth,
ii. inheritance from ancestors and
iii. by ordinary residency since at least five years before commencement of the Constitution of India, viz., January 26, 1950.

Article 6 defines any immigrant from Pakistan to be considered Indian Citizen with commencement of the Constitution of India under certain conditions. Such conditions include –

Birth of
i. either of the parents

Or

ii. Either of the grandparent
- in territory of India as defined under sections of Government of India Act, 1935,
    a. If the immigrant in question migrated to India before July 19, 1948 and did not leave India since,

and

b. If such immigrants migrated between July 19, 1948 and January 26, 1950 and applied in prescribed form to the

Government of India appointed officer as Citizen of Dominion of India and remained resident of Dominion of India at least for six prior months from applying for Indian Citizenship.

Article 8 elaborates citizenships for the persons residing outside territory of India as defined under sections of Government of India Act of 1935 under conditions. Such conditions include –

   i. birth of either of the parents in India,

   Or

   ii. the grandparents being resident of India defined under sections of Government of India Act of 1935

   and -

   registration of such person to be citizen of India by the diplomatic or consular representative at the person's country of residence against the application by the person on forms provided by -

   a. the Government of Dominion of India before January 26, 1950

   Or

   b. the Government of India after January 26, 1950[1].

Article 7 and Article 9 defines who cannot be a citizen of India.

---

[1] Government of India, 1950. *The Constitution of India.* [Online] Available at:https://www.india.gov.in/sites/upload_files/npi/files/coi_part_full.pdf [Accessed 27 February 2020].

Article 7 excludes any person migrating from India to Pakistan on or after March 1, 1947, even if the person was born in India, or either of the parents or the grandparents of the person was born in India. Yet, if a person, who has –

- migrated to Pakistan after March 1, 1947 from India,
- returned to India under a permit of resettlement or permanent return issued by any legal authority, -

then the person in question is considered to be citizen of India who –

- migrated to India after July 19, 1948 and
- is registered by an officer appointed by the Government of India against application of the person submitted before January 26, 1950 and
- residing in India for at least six months prior to submitting an application for registration.

Article 9 unequivocally pronounces that any person acquiring citizenship of another country voluntarily shall not remain a citizen of India even if that person could have been considered to be Indian citizen by provisions of Article 5, Article 6 and Article 8.

Article 10 ensures continuity of citizenship. Any person, if being a citizen of India under provisions of Part II of the Constitution of India shall remain to be Indian citizens, *unless* provisions of any law made by the Parliament makes the person cease to be Indian citizen.

Article 11 *vests right in the Parliament for making laws regarding citizenship*, its acquisition and termination.

These provisions were made prior to framing of the Citizenship Act (1955). These were working principles of defining citizenship of India in absence of an Act suitable for the purpose. These articles were also for determining eligibility of citizenship of persons migrating to Pakistan (including the country, which is now Bangladesh, but was Pakistan then) and migrating back to India. These articles have been enshrined and elaborated in the Citizenship Act (1955). Abiding by Article 10 of the constitution of India, amendments of the Citizenship Act (1955) have also framed provisions for cessations of Indian citizenship.

The Citizenship Act, 1955 as Amended

Based on the constitutional framework discussed in the preceding chapter came the Citizenship Act, 1955. Salient features of this acts are enumerated as follows:

- **Section 1** clarifies that the act of citizenship in India can be called the Citizenship Act, 1955.
- **Section 2** clarifies several phrases as used in this Act through its four subsections.
  - Subsection (1) comprises interpretation of different terms like Government, Indian Consulate, Overseas Citizen of India et cetera under different clauses.
    - ❖ It has defined "a Government of India" to be the Central Government or a State Government. [clause (a)]
    - ❖ Definition of illegal migrant was inserted as clause (b) of Section 2 subsection (1) by amendments of 2004 in Section. Illegal migrant is defined as a person who has entered India either without valid passport and travel documents or overstayed visa period when entered with valid passport and relevant travel documents.

This clause (b) of subsection (1) Section (2) has been amended by *Citizenship (Amendment) Act, 2019*. It has enabled the Central Government to exempt certain persons to be categorized as illegal migrants on a case-by-case basis, not as general exceptions for all. The conditions laid out for allowing exemptions for such persons are as follows:

1. The person must belong to any of the following religions:
   - Hindu
   - Sikh
   - Buddhist
   - Jain
   - Parsi
   - Christian

2. They must enter from one of the following countries:
   \> Afghanistan
   \> Pakistan
   \> Bangladesh
3. They must enter India on or before December 31, 2014.
4. They must be exempted by the Central Government -

   - by or under clause (c) of subsection (2) of section 3 of Passport (Entry into India) Act, 1920 which speaks for conditional or absolute exemption under rules made by the Central Government regarding passport issuing and renewing authority of persons entering India
   OR
   - from the application of the provisions of the Foreigners Act, 1946 or any order or rule made under this act.

All these conditions together must be satisfied for being exempted to be considered as illegal migrants.

- ❖ Clause (b) and clause (c) of subsection (1) of Section 2 in discussion were entirely substituted by Act 6 of 2004 sec. 2 with effect from 3 December 2004.[2]
- ❖ Clause (d) defines the "Indian Consulate" being any consular office of the Government of India where a register of birth is kept. Or, where there exists no consular office of the Government of India, any office prescribed for registration of birth would be considered Indian Consulate for the purpose of the Act in discussion.
- ❖ A "minor" has been defined in clause (e) as a person younger than eighteen years of age. Thus, any person of "full age" is eighteen years or older.

---

[2]Government of India, 2021. [Online] Available at: https://indiancitizenshiponline.nic.in/UserGuide/Citizenship_Act_1955_16042019.pdf, [Accessed on June 1, 2021.]

- ❖ Overseas Citizen of India (OCI) is a person registered by the Government of India to be OCI under Section 7A of Citizenship Act, 1955. This provision is the result of amendments of CAA, 2005 vide sec. 2(1) (ee) of the Citizenship Act, 1955.
- ❖ By definition of clause (f) person excludes the followings:
  - Any company
  - Association
  - Body of individuals
    - incorporated or not.
- ❖ Clause (g) defines "prescribed" as prescribed by the rules made under this Act.
- ❖ CAA, 2005 has omitted clause (gg) of subsection (1) of Section 2. It was about interpretation of specified countries as mentioned in the Fourth Schedule. Fourth Schedule, too, was omitted by the same amendment. It used to comprise sixteen countries till omission. The sixteen countries have been listed as follows:
  1. Australia,
  2. Canada,
  3. Finland,
  4. France,
  5. Greece,
  6. Ireland,
  7. Israel,
  8. Italy,
  9. Netherlands,
  10. New Zealand,
  11. Portugal,
  12. Republic of Cyprus,
  13. Sweden,
  14. Switzerland,
  15. United Kingdom and
  16. United States of America.

These were inserted only by Act 6 of 2004, section 19 and remained effective from December 3, 2004, to June 28, 2005, i.e., only for almost six months. Clause (gg) of Sec. 2(1) of the Citizenship Act, 1955, had provisions for insertion and deletion of countries into erstwhile Fourth Schedule by the Central Government by means of issuing notifications in the official gazette with condition that such notifications must be laid before each Houses of the Parliament.

Under that now abandoned clause, Overseas Citizen of India used to be defined as a person of Indian origin born in any one of those countries in Fourth Schedule or a person who was an Indian citizen immediately before accepting citizenship of any one of those countries listed in Fourth Schedule.

It was a narrow definition for OCI as it was limited to only a few countries. Now, the scope of definition of OCI is quite broader.

However, CAA of 2005 explained that the Fourth Schedule was omitted to expand the scope of granting Overseas Citizenship of India to Persons of Indian Origin of all countries except Pakistan and Bangladesh.

- ❖ In clause (h) "undivided India" has been defined to be India defined in the Government of India Act, 1935 as originally enacted.

Observation:
The entire subsection has put a lot of effort into clarify the critical terms used in the Act.
- Subsection (2) of Sec. 2 defines the citizenship of persons born abroad registered aircraft and ship or abroad unregistered aircraft and ship of the Government of any country. The citizenship of such

persons shall be of the place or country to which the aircraft or ship is being registered.
- Subsection (3) of the section in discussion, spells out the status or description of father of person at the time of birth of the person for the purpose of the Act, viz., the Citizenship Act, 1955, especially if such person is born posthumously. This subsection pronounces that the status of father at the time of death would be considered as the status of the father if the death of the father occurred before the commencement of the Act and the birth of the person occurred after the commencement of the Citizenship Act (1955). Also, this subsection pronounces that, status or description of a father of a posthumously born person, if father died after the commencement of the Citizenship Act (1955), would be considered as the status or description of the father at the time of father's death. Here all considerations are about the citizenship status of a father of a posthumously born person.
- Subsection (4) defines how this Act, viz., the Citizenship Act of India, considers a person of full age and capacity. It considers a person of full age if the person is not a Minor. It considers a person of full capacity if the person is not of unsound mind.

Sections 3 through 7 define various ways of acquiring citizenship of India. These are as follows:

- **Section 3** spells out provisions of citizenship *by birth*. This section of the original act of 1955 was totally substituted by amendments of 2004, incorporating amendments of 2003. Subsection (1) of this section defines different conditions of birth of Indian citizens. Subsection (2) pronounces the conditions that **deprive** a person to be a citizen of India though born in India.
  - ❖ There are 3 (three) clauses under subsection (1)[3]. These clauses define eligibility of citizenship for

---

[3]Government of India, 1955. *The Citizenship Act, 1955.* [Online] Available

persons born in India with respect to their respective dates of birth belonging to a range of dates in definition. These dates are as follows:

- *On or after January 26, 1950, and before July 1, 1987,* vide sec. 3 (1) (a) of the Citizenship Act, 1955; due to this clause several tourists' offspring could become citizens of India until amendments of 1987 suggested otherwise.
- *On or after July 1, 1987, but before commencement of CAA, 2003,* i.e., December 3, 2004, vide sec. 3 (1) (b) of the Citizenship Act, 1955. People born in this range of dates *must have at least one parent to be Indian citizen at the time of birth.* Due to this clause, offspring of one illegal immigrant married to an Indian citizen was eligible for Indian citizenship until amendments of 2003.

- *On or after commencement of CAA, 2003,* i.e., December 3, 2004, [sec. 3 (1) (c) of the Citizenship Act, 1955] under two conditions defined under two subclauses as follows:
  - If *both parents* of the person born on or after commencement of CAA, 2003 and seeking citizenship of India *are Indian citizens* [sec. 3 (1) (c) (i) of the Citizenship Act, 1955]
  - If at least one parent is Indian citizen and the other parent is **not** an illegal migrant of the person born on or after commencement of CAA, 2003 and seeking citizenship of India [sec. 3 (1) (c) (ii) of the Citizenship Act, 1955]

Observation:

This is the first instance where citizenship is denied to offspring of illegal migrant.

---

at:https://indiacode.nic.in/bitstream/123456789/4210/1/Citizenship_Act_1955.pdf [Accessed 27 February 2020]

- ❖ There are 2 (two) clauses under subsection 2. This subsection pronounces conditions that **deprive a person** born in India of Indian citizenship. The conditions are as follows:
  - ▪ A person *born in India is not an Indian citizen if* the person is born to parents who are or at least one parent who is enjoying immunity from legal processes due to some accord between the President of India and representatives of foreign sovereign power.
  - ▪ A person is born to citizens of an enemy nation while the enemy nation was occupying Indian Territory.

  Observation:
  This is the process of denying citizenship to offspring of foreigners who violated laws of the land.

- **Section 4** provides for citizenship *by descent*[4]. Two of three original subsections of this section remain intact while subsection (1) has been totally substituted by CAA of 2004 [vide Act 6 of 2004, sec. 4, for subsection (1) (with effect from December 3, 2004)].
  - ❖ Sub-section (1) through several clauses defines how a person born outside India can be considered Indian citizen.
    - ▪ A person, born outside India between January 26, 1950 and December 10, 1992, can be considered a citizen of India if the person's father remains citizen of India at the time of birth [sec. 4 (1) (a) of the Citizenship Act, 1955].
    - ▪ If father of the person to be considered citizen of India is himself a citizen by descent, then the birth of the person must be registered at an Indian consulate within one year of birth or the

---

[4]Government of India, 1955. *The Citizenship Act, 1955*. [Online] Available at:https://indiacode.nic.in/bitstream/123456789/4210/1/Citizenship_Act_1 955.pdf [Accessed 28 February 2020]

commencement of the act, viz, the Citizenship Act, 1955 and its subsequent amendments, which of the two is later. Such registration needs permission of the Central Government after expiry of aforementioned one-year period.
- Otherwise, if the father in question is in service under the Government of India.

Observation:

This original segment of the Act must have meant parent by the term "father". Even in the nineteen fifties Indian Foreign Service used to recruit women. (Rathore, 2020) Vijay Lakshmi Pandit was the first female ambassador of India to the Soviet Union. She was appointed in 1947. C.B. Muthamma was the first female Indian Foreign Service Office. She was appointed in 1949 and fought hard through her way to the hierarchy inducing changes in the discriminatory service rules.

- The scope of parents being citizens of India at the time birth of a person applying for Indian citizenship has been broadened in this subclause. It pronounces that persons born on or after December 10, 1992 having at least one parent being an Indian Citizen will be considered citizen of India [sec. 4 (1)(b) of the Citizenship Act, 1955].
  - If the parents of the person to be considered a citizen of India is himself a citizen by descent, then the birth of the person must be registered at an Indian consulate within one year of birth or on or after December 10, 1992, which of the two is later. Later registration of birth is possible only with permission of the Government of India.
  - Otherwise, if, at least one parent of the person in question is in service under the Government of India.

Observation:
This segment of law is about birth of citizen after 1992. It mentions "parent"/ "parents" instead of "father". Hence, change did happen.

- Also, on or after commencement of CAA 2003, to be Indian citizen by descent, a person outside India must have birth registered at Indian Consulate by prescribed forms within one year from birth or after commencement of CAA 2003, which happens later. The person needs permission from the Central Government to become Indian citizen if birth is not registered within the aforementioned one-year period.
- Moreover, a person born outside India can obtain Indian citizenship by descent if either of the parents declares in prescribed form that the person in question does not hold a passport of any other country

Observation:
The above clauses does not explicitly mention if the parents could have passports of another country whose offspring is seeking citizenship of India.

- ❖ Subsection 1(A) defines how a person born outside India can lose Indian citizenship by descent. If such person, while being a citizen of India by descent, is a minor and holds citizenship of any other country then the person ceases to be Indian citizen after attaining full age unless the person renounces citizenship and nationality of the other country.
- ❖ Subsection (2) pronounces the power of the Central Government for giving permission for registration of birth of a person who can be considered to be citizen of India by descent under subsections of sec. 4 (1) (b) of the Citizenship Act, 1955.
- ❖ Subsection (3) pronounces those persons born outside undivided India are only considered citizens by

descent since commencement of Constitution of India for all conditions stated under Section 4 (1) (b) of the Citizenship Act, 1955. Before December 10, 1992, this subsection was only applicable for male persons. This subsection used to exclude females to be Indian citizens by descent under Section 4 (1) (b) of the Citizenship Act, 1955.

This section provides some flexibility for registration of birth of persons seeking Indian citizenship through intervention of the Central Government.

- **Section 5** lays out the provisions for citizenship *by registration*[5]. This section comprises six subsections. They are as follows:
  ❖ Sub-section (1) is about the person seeking citizenship of India by registration. This sub-section has been substituted by Act 6 of 2004. The substitution came into effect on December 3, 2004. Under different conditions only the Central Government can register a person to be Indian citizen for people applying for such citizenship if the applicant is not an Indian citizen by virtue of other provisions of the Indian Citizenship Act, 1955 as amended or the applicant is not an illegal migrant. The other conditions for applying to register as Indian Citizen are laid down under several clauses as follows:
  ▫ Applicant is a person of Indian origin ordinarily residing in India for seven years before making application for registration. [sec. 5 (1) (a) of the Citizenship Act, 1955]

---

[5]Government of India, 1955. *The Citizenship Act, 1955.* [Online] Available at:https://indiacode.nic.in/bitstream/123456789/4210/1/Citizenship_Act_1 955.pdf [Accessed 3 March 2020]

- Applicant is a person of Indian origin ordinarily residing in any country or place outside undivided India. [sec. 5 (1) (b) of the Citizenship Act, 1955]
- Applicant is a person married to an Indian Citizen and is residing in India ordinarily for seven years before applying for citizenship by registration. [sec. 5 (1) (c) of the Citizenship Act, 1955]
- Minor children of Indian citizens [sec. 5 (1) (d) of the Citizenship Act, 1955]
- Applicant is a full aged person whose parents happen to be citizens by registration vide clause (a) of subsection (1) of section 5 and subsection (1) of section 6 of the Citizenship Act, 1955 as amended. [sec. 5 (1) (e) of the Citizenship Act, 1955]
- Applicant was an Indian citizen or applicant's parents were Indian citizen and the applicant has been residing ordinarily for at least twelve months before applying for such citizenship. [sec. 5 (1) (f) of the Citizenship Act, 1955]

The condition of "ordinary residency of twelve months" has been a substitution for "residency for one year" by CAA, 2015[6].

- Applicant is of full age and capacity has already been registered as Overseas Citizen of India Cardholder for at least five years and already residing in India for at least one year can apply for registration as Indian citizen. The condition of residing in India ordinarily for twelve months prior to applying for registration is a substitution by CAA, 2005, sec. 3 for two years.

CAA, 2015 has substituted "Overseas Citizen of India" in the parent act, viz., the Citizenship Act, 1955 by "Overseas Citizen of India Cardholder". Also, the condition of

---

[6]Government of India, 1955. *The Citizenship (Amendment) Act, 2015.* [Online] Available at: https://indiancitizenshiponline.nic.in/UserGuide/E-gazette.pdf [Accessed on April 27, 2020.]

"residency of one year" has been substituted by "ordinary residency of twelve months" by the same amendments.

This subsection comes with two explanations. They are as follows:

- ❖ Subsection (1A) empowers the Central Government to relax the period of twelve months to up to a maximum of thirty days. These thirty days can be in different breaks. Before allowing relaxation, the Central Government must be satisfied that special circumstances exist with respect to an applicant and such circumstances must be recorded in writing. However, such relaxation is applicable to clauses (f), (g) and clause (i) of Explanation 1, hence on clauses (a) and (c) as Explanation 1 is related to these clauses. This subsection has been inserted by CAA, 2015.

In this entire section "ordinarily" is explained as residing twelve months immediately before applying for registration [as mentioned in clause (i) of Explanation 1] and at least six years of a period of eight years immediately preceding aforementioned twelve months [as mentioned in clause (ii) of Explanation 1]. Also, a person of Indian origin has been explained [Explanation 2] as a person or either of the person's parents being born in undivided India or in territories which became part of India after August 15, 1947.

- ❖ The persons to be registered as Indian citizen must take oath of allegiance as specified in Second Schedule of the Citizenship Act, 1955 as amended vide sec. 5 (2) of the Citizenship Act, 1955]
- ❖ The persons whose Indian citizenship was terminated or a person who has renounced Indian citizenship or somehow has been deprived of Indian citizenship can never obtain Indian citizenship by registration with exception of order of the Central Government. [sec. 5 (3) of the Citizenship Act, 1955]

- ❖ The Central Government, if satisfied with special circumstances, may grant minors citizenship by registration. [sec. 5 (4) of the Citizenship Act, 1955]
- ❖ The date of commencement of citizenship of a person who has obtained citizenship by registration is the date of registration under sections of the Citizenship Act, 1955 as amended. If a person is an Indian citizen by registration vide clause (b)(ii) of Article 6 or Article 8 of Constitution of India, then date of commencement of citizenship of such person is date of commencement of the Constitution of India or the date of registration which one is later. [sec. 5 (5) of the Citizenship Act, 1955]
- ❖ The Central Government has discretion in matter of being lenient on period of residency in India as mentioned in clause (c) of subsection (1) of the Citizenship Act, 1955 as amended, if the Central Government is satisfied with circumstances that makes it necessary to exempt the mandatory residency period for person or class of persons applying for Indian citizenship by registration. [sec. 5 (6) of the Citizenship Act, 1955]

Observation:

The Central government is the sole authority in matters of citizenship by registration.

- **Section 6** provides options for citizenship *by naturalization*. This provision under section 6 of the Citizenship Act, 1955 appears to be the only provision that has remained mostly unaltered since 1955. The only substitution was in subsection (1) in 2004 vide Act 6 of 2004. This amendment has substituted the phrase "who is not a citizen of a country specified in the First Schedule" by "not being an illegal migrant". Thus, the provision was elaborated in aforesaid First Schedule has widely been amended. At present, the conditions of naturalization under the subsection (1) of Section 6 of

the Citizenship Act, 1955 as amended, has been elaborated under the Third Schedule. The provisions of citizenship have been defined through two subsections as follows:
- Under subsection (1) of Section 6 of the Citizenship Act, 1955 as amended, the Central Government is empowered to grant certificate of naturalization to the applicants of full age and capacity –
  1. if such applicant is not an illegal migrant
  2. if application of naturalization has been made in prescribed format
  3. if the Central Government is satisfied that the applicant is qualified for naturalization under provisions of the Third Schedule

  Observation:
  All above conditions hold only if the applicants are of full age and capacity.
- The Central Government can waive all or any of the conditions defined in the Third Schedule if the Central Government accepts the applicants as distinguished performers of services to the cause of science, philosophy, art, literature, world peace or human progress generally.
- Subsection (2) of Section 6 of the Citizenship Act, 1955 as amended, mentions that grant of certificate of naturalization does not make an applicant of such citizenship a citizen of India. After an applicant receives a certificate of naturalization, the applicant needs to take an oath of allegiance in prescribed format to become citizens of India on the date of issue of certificate of naturalization. Oath of allegiance is in the Second Schedule of the Citizenship Act, 1955 as amended.
- Third Schedule of the Citizenship Act, 1955 as amended has laid out qualifications of naturalization as follows:

- The applicant cannot be a citizen of any country that prevents Indian citizens, by law or practice, from becoming a naturalized citizen in that country.
- The applicant, if, is a citizen of another country, then, is required to undertake to renounce such citizenship as soon as the applicant applies for citizenship of India by naturalization.
- The applicant needs to reside in India throughout a period of twelve months immediately prior to the date of application. This residency over the aforementioned twelve months period can be a residency legally or in service of a Government in India or partly both. CAA, 2015 has inserted here that the Central Government can relax the period of twelve months if it is satisfied of the existence of special circumstances and recorded the matter in writing. Such relaxation can maximum be of thirty days. Such thirty days can be in different breaks.
- The applicant must reside in India legally before commencement of aforesaid twelve months period for at least fourteen years. Otherwise, the applicant may reside in India or in service of a Government in India or partly both for a total period of at least eleven years. The periods of fourteen years and eleven years have been substituted respectively for twelve years and nine years by section 18 of Act 6 of 20004 and came in effect on December 3, 2004.

CAA, 2019 has amended the third schedule. Its Section 6 has added a condition that for the persons belonging to Hindu, Sikh, Buddhist, Jain, Parsi or Christian communities in Afghanistan, Bangladesh or Pakistan the aggregate period of residence in India or aggregate period of service to any state or the Central Government in India has been reduced from eleven years to five years.

- The applicant must be of good character.

- The applicant must have adequate knowledge of a language specified in the Eighth Schedule of the Constitution of India. There are twenty-two languages in the Eighth Schedule of the Constitution of India. These are (1) Assamese, (2) Bengali, (3) Gujarati, (4) Hindi, (5) Kannada, (6) Kashmiri, (7) Konkani, (8) Malayalam, (9) Manipuri, (10) Marathi, (11) Nepali, (12) Oriya, (13) Punjabi, (14) Sanskrit, (15) Sindhi, (16) Tamil, (17) Telugu, (18) Urdu (19) Bodo, (20) Santhali, (21) Maithili and (22) Dogri.
- The Central Government may allow under special circumstances, if it thinks fit -
  - A continuous period of twelve months ending at most six months before reckoning of application of citizenship by naturalization instead of twelve months period immediately before date of application as mentioned earlier.
  - A period of fifteen years before the date of application to be reckoned for calculating the total period of residency of applicant in India.
  - Only If the applicant intends to continue to –
  - reside in India, or to be in service of a Government in India, or
  - be in service of an international organization which has India as its member, or
  - to be in service of a society, company, body of persons established in India.

Observation:

Issue of illegal migration has been dealt legally as late as in 2004[7]. Therefore, under present paradigm of country wide NRC and NPR, the resistance to illegal immigration

---

[7]Government of India, 1955. *The Citizenship Act, 1955*. [Online] Available at:https://indiacode.nic.in/bitstream/123456789/4210/1/Citizenship_Act_1 955.pdf [Accessed 4 March 2020]

(migration) is not at all a new thought in Indian legislative minds (broadly speaking, in Indian minds).
- **Section 6A** spells out citizenship *by special provisions covered by Assam Accord*.[8] This section was inserted by amendment of 1985 vide Act 65 of 1985, sec. 2. This section came into effect on December 7, 1985. This appears to be a complete law itself with its own definitions of certain terms under clauses of Subsection (1). It comprises eight (8) subsections. These are detailed as follows:
  - ❖ Subsection (1) Comprises of five definitions under five different clauses. These are as follows:
    - ▢ Assam is the territory included in the state of Assam immediately before commencement of the Citizenship (Amendment) Act, 1985 [sec. 6A (1) (a) of the Citizenship Act, 1955 as amended]
    - ▢ Foreigner is defined under the provisions of the Foreigners Act 1946 (31 of 1946) and the Foreigners Tribunal Order 1964 by a Tribunal constituted under the aforesaid order [sec. 6A (1) (b) of the Citizenship Act, 1955 as amended]
    - ▢ Territories included in Bangladesh immediately before commencement of
    CAA, 1985 are 'specified territories' [sec. 6A (1) (c) of the Citizenship Act, 1955 as amended]
    - ▢ A person, either of whose parents or any of whose grandparents was born in undivided India shall be considered as of Indian origin [sec. 6A (1) (d) of the Citizenship Act, 1955 as amended]
    - ▢ A foreigner would be detected when the Tribunal constituted under Foreigners Tribunal Order 1964 submits its opinion to the effect to the appropriate

---

[8]Government of India, 1955. *The Citizenship Act, 1955.* [Online] Available at:https://indiacode.nic.in/bitstream/123456789/4210/1/Citizenship_Act_1955.pdf [Accessed 5,7,9,10 March 2020]

authority [sec. 6A (1) (e) of the Citizenship Act, 1955 as amended]

All phrases seemingly vague at this point are going to be crystal clear at the end of the section if reading continues.

❖ Subsection (2) defines how denizens of Assam can be defined as Citizen of India on and after January 1, 1966 -
  - if their residency abides by provisions of Sub-sections (6) and (7) of Section 6A of the Citizenship Act, 1955 as amended
  - if they are of Indian Origin as defined under Sec. 6A(1)(d) of the Citizenship Act, 1955 as amended
  - if they entered India from Bangladesh, as defined in Sec. 6A (1) (c) of the Citizenship Act, 1955 as amended, before January 1, 1966, even if, their names were included in the electoral roll for the purpose of the General Election of the House of People (Lok Sabha / Lower house of Parliament) held in 1967
  - if they have been ordinary residents of Assam, as defined by Sec. 6A (1) (a) of the Citizenship Act, 1955 as amended, since the dates of their entry to Assam

❖ Subsection (3) delineates the principles to root out the foreigners from electoral roll -

- Even if such persons abide by Sub-sections (6) and (7) of Section 6A of the Citizenship Act, 1955 as amended

-If such persons entered Assam, defined under 6A(1)(a) of the Citizenship Act, 1955, after January 1, 1966, but before March 25, 1971, from Bangladesh as defined in Sec. 6A (1) (c) of the Citizenship Act, 1955

- if such persons remained ordinary residents of Assam since their entry

- if such persons were detected to be foreigners as defined under sec. 6A (1) (e) of the Citizenship Act, 1955 as amended

Prior to deletion of their name from electoral roll, these persons must register themselves in accordance with the rules of the Central Government made under Section 18 of the Citizenship Act, 1955 as amended in this matter. This subsection vests sole power of decision making regarding identifying a person as foreigner in the Central Government. For such identification, the Central Government makes required and relevant rules under aforementioned Section 18.

This section was framed in 1985. Then Bangladesh was an existing nation. But during the reference periods of migration viz. between January 1, 1966, and March 25, 1971, and during the year of the Foreigner (Tribunals) Order viz., 1964, Bangladesh was not constituted and used to be referred as East Pakistan or Pakistan. Probably for avoiding scopes of misunderstanding, the territories from which migration from January 1, 1966, to March 25, 1971, are mentioned in this section, were mentioned as 'specified territories', instead of mentioning a nation's name or the other.

- ❖ Subsection (4) utters the limit of the period during which a foreigner can have Indian passport yet cannot be included in the electoral roll. That time is ten year long from acquiring foreigner status under provisions of subsection (3). During these ten years, people designated as foreigners would have the same rights and obligations as Indian citizens, including acquiring a passport under provisions of the Passport Act, 1967 (15 of 1967) and its consequent obligations.
- ❖ Subsection (5) mentions how long a foreigner needs to become a citizen of India. It is specified that on expiry of ten years after the date of registration as a

foreigner, a person is considered to be an Indian citizen.
- ❖ Subsection (6) suggests ways to renounce Indian citizenship even after being accepted as a citizen of India under subsections of the current section in discussion. These are as follows:
  - ▣ Residents of Assam who wished not to be Indian citizens under subsection (2) of current section in discussion, can submit in prescribed format to the Central Government within sixty days from the date of commencement of Citizenship (Amendment) Act 1985 and renounce their respective Indian citizenships.
  - ▣ Any foreigners identified under Subsection (3) of the section in discussion, can express wish for not being considered to be Indian citizen or abide by provisions of Subsections (3), (4) and (5). Such persons require to submit their wish in prescribed format to the Central Government within sixty days from commencement of CAA, 1985 or from the date the person has been detected to be foreigner, whichever is later, and the person shall no longer require to register to be foreigner under provisions of the section in discussion, viz. 6A of the Citizenship Act, 1955.

  The above clause simplifies the complications over identifying foreigners under provisions of the current section in discussion.
- ❖ Subsection (7) spells out conditions to rule out persons from considerations under provisions of subsections (2) to (6) of Section 6A of the Citizenship Act, 1955 as amended. These conditions are as follows:
  - ▣ Persons who were Indian citizens immediately before commencement of CAA, 1985

- Persons expelled from India under provisions of Foreigners Act, 1946 before commencement of CAA, 1985.

  These are the two boundary conditions to be exempted from provisions under subsections and clauses for identifying foreigners in Assam.
- ❖ Subsection (8) overrules all other legal provisions in the matter of residents of Assam being considered to be Indian Citizens, until further amendment of this section and the Citizenship Act, 1955.

CAA, 2019 has inserted **Section 6B** to the principal act, viz., the Citizenship Act, 1955 (Sec. 3 of CAA, 2019). It has four subsections. These are amendments to Sec 6 and Sec. 6A in connection with amended clause (b) of subsection (1) of Sec. 2 of the principal act. The subsections of Sec. 6B are detailed as follows:

- Subsection (1) is about issuing *certificate of naturalization* to persons who will be exempted from being illegal immigrants by provisions of Sec 2(1)(b) amended by CAA, 2019. The certificate of naturalization will be issued to the persons who will apply in prescribed forms to the Central Government, or an authority specified by it.
- Subsection (2) defines the date of citizenship for the persons who have issued certificate of naturalization or certificate of registration under provisions of clause (b) subsection (1) Section 2 as amended by CAA, 2019 after -
  - Fulfilling conditions of specified in Section 5 of the principal act

  Or
  - Being qualified for naturalization under the provisions of the Third Schedule

  Date of commencement of citizenship of such persons will be the date of entry to India.
- Subsection (3) defers decision on status of being illegal migrant in India or being citizen of India as CAA,

2019 comes in effect depending on following conditions:
➢ If an applicant is found qualified to be Indian citizen under provisions of this section, then that applicant's application cannot be rejected by the Central Government or authority specified by it on the ground that proceedings on such applicant's application remains pending.
➢ The applicants eligible for citizenship under provisions of this section must not be deprived of their rights and privileges while waiting for decision on their applications.

▫ Subsection (4) asserts the areas exempted from jurisdiction of this section. These are –
> Tribal areas of, as included in the Sixth Schedule of the Constitution of India,
      -Assam
      -Meghalaya-
      -Mizoram
      -Tripura
> The area covered under "The Inner Line" notified under the Bengal Eastern Frontier Regulation, 1873.
Because of its huge volume and structure, Section 6A could have stood out as an Act itself.

- **Section 7** is about citizenship *by incorporation of Territory*[9]. By virtue of this provision, when new territory is included in the Union of India, the Central Government publishes notification in the official gazette about its *order specifying* the persons who can be citizens of India. The reasons for these persons being Indian citizens can be their connection to the aforementioned territory. The commencement of

---

[9]Government of India, 1955. *The Citizenship Act, 1955.* [Online] Available at:https://indiacode.nic.in/bitstream/123456789/4210/1/Citizenship_Act_1955.pdf [Accessed 3 March 2020]

citizenship of those persons are mentioned in the aforesaid order of the Central Government.

Observation:

Amendments of 1987, 2003 and 2004 have gradually shrunken the scope of becoming Indian citizens. Amendments of 1987 prevented any foreigners giving birth in India asking for citizenship of India for the child born in India. Act of 2003 prevented illegal immigrants' children to become citizen of India.[10]

Sections 7A through 7D deals with *Overseas Citizens of India.* All provisions in the matter of overseas citizenship of India have been inserted by Sec 7 of Act 6 of 2004. These became effective on December 12, 2004. However, Section 7A lasted only for six months till June 28, 2005, when Section 4 of the Citizenship (Amendment) Act, 2005 came into effect. Section 4 of the Citizenship (Amendment) Act, 2005 substituted erstwhile Section 7A entirely. However, all sections, 7A through 7D have been substituted by CAA, 2015. The provisions of Sections 7A through 7D are discussed through following paragraphs.

- **Section 7A** defines the processes of Registration of Overseas Citizen of India Cardholder. According to the Citizenship (Amendment) Act, 2005, Section 7A comprises two subsections. These are explained as follows:
  ❖ Subsection (1) of section 7A comprises two clauses. The first clause is constituted of four subclauses. These are as follows:
    ▫ Under prescribed restrictions and conditions, the Central Government can register an applicant seeking to become Overseas Citizens of India Cardholder as overseas citizen of India if the applicant is -
    ▫ A person of full age and capacity [Section 7A (1) (a)] and -

---

[10] Same as previous, i.e., 9 [Accessed 12 March 2020]

1. The person is a citizen of another country but used to be citizen of India at the time of or any time after commencement of the constitution [Section 7A (1) (a) (i)].
2. The person is a citizen of another country but was eligible to become citizen of India at the time of commencement of the Constitution of India [Section 7A (1) (a) (ii)].
3. The person is a citizen of another country but belongs to territory that became part of the Union of India after August 15, 1947[Section 7A (1) (a) (iii)].
4. Or a child or grandchild or great-grandchild of persons conferred with overseas citizenship of India [Section 7A (1) (a) (iv)].

The above subclauses are only applicable to persons of full age and capacity.

- A person is minor and is the offspring of another person who is an Overseas Citizen of India as laid through clause (a) of subsection (1) of section 7A [Section 7A (1) (b)].
- A person is minor and the person's both parents are Indian citizens or one of the parents is Indian citizen [Section 7A (1) (c)].
- Spouse of foreign origin of a citizen of India or an Overseas Citizen of India Cardholder under section 7A whose marriage has been registered and subsisted for a continuous period of at least two years prior to presentation of the application under this section under following conditions:

1. Such spouses would be subjected to prior security clearance by competent authority of India.
2. Overseas Citizenship of India Cardholders status is not conferred to citizens of Pakistan, Bangladesh and some other countries as ordered by the Central Government through notifications published in the official gazette [Section 7A (1) (d)].

Quite overtly citizens of Pakistan and Bangladesh are declined to be Overseas Citizenship of India Cardholders.

- ❖ Subsection (2) bestowed power on the Central Government for specifying date from which the existing Persons of Indian Origin Cardholders may be deemed to be Overseas Citizen of India Cardholders. The Central Government must make notifications on its official gazette while specifying such date. The definition of Persons of Indian Origin Cardholders is persons registered as Persons of Indian Origin Cardholders under notifications issued by the Central Government [notification number 26011/ 4/98 F.I., dated the 19th of August 2002].
- ❖ Subsection (3) empowers the Central Government to register a person as Overseas Citizen of India Cardholder irrespective of conditions laid in Subsection (1) in this section, if it is satisfied that special circumstances exist and records existence of special circumstances in writing.

Overseas Citizen of India were entitled to a few rights specified by the Central Government which were revoked by CAA, 2015. These were –

a) Grant of multiple entry lifelong visa for visiting India for any purpose.
b) Exemption from registration with Foreign Regional Registration officer or Foreign Registration Officer for any duration of stay in India.
c) Equal treatment compared to Non-resident Indians with respect to all facilities available to Overseas Citizens of India in economic, financial and educational fields leaving matters of acquiring agricultural or plantations properties[11].

Section 7A in the Act 6 of 2004, s.7, at first inception of eligibility conditions of registration of Overseas Indian

---

[11]S.O. 542 (E) dated 11th April 2005 Gazette of India Extra Pt. II Sec. 3 (ii) dated 11th April 2005

Citizens, comprised three subsections. Subsection (1), defined under given restrictions and conditions of mutual benefit, the Central Government was empowered to register applicants overseas Indian citizenship if the applicant is –
a) Of Indian origin and of full age and capacity and citizen of a specified country.
b) Of full age and capacity and became citizen of a specified country on or after commencement of the Citizenship (Amendment) Act, 2003 and was citizen of India immediately before commencement of the aforesaid act.
c) A minor child of persons described through preceding paragraphs.

Clearly the scope of becoming Overseas Citizen of India has been widened through the Citizenship (Amendment) Act, 2005. The definition timeline has been moved back to the days of commencement of Constitution of India (January 26, 1950) and Independence of India on August 15, 1947. However, the section 7A under the Citizenship (Amendment) Act, 2004 explained that a person of Indian Origin is –
a) A person who was eligible of becoming Indian citizen at the commencement of the Constitution of India, i.e., on January 26, 1950.
b) A person belonged to a territory that became part of the Union of India after August 15, 1947.
c) A person who is child or grandchild of a person of Indian Origin as described in preceding paragraphs but not a person who is citizen of Pakistan and/or Bangladesh and/or any other countries specified by the Central Government by order published in its official gazette.

Observation:
Therefore, this explanation apart from the amendment of 2004 has almost entirely become stricture in the Citizenship (Amendment) Act, 2005. However, it

remained silent about the condition of excluding citizens of Pakistan, Bangladesh and other specified countries from becoming overseas citizens of India.

Observation:

Section 7 subsection (2) of the Citizenship (Amendment) Act, 2004 specified the date of commencement of overseas citizenship of applicants described in Subsection (1) would be the date of registration. The latter act, viz., the Citizenship (Amendment) Act, 2005 has not specified any such date of commencement of overseas citizenship of applicants. Rather, it has been left in utter ambiguity.

Section 7 subsection (3) of the Citizenship (Amendment) Act, 2004 pronounced that any person deprived of Indian citizenship under provisions of sections of the Citizenship Act, 1955 as amended till then was ineligible of becoming an Overseas citizen of India unless the Central Government makes an exception by an order. The subsequent act, viz., of the Citizenship (Amendment) Act, 2005 does not have this provision. It remains ambiguous in this matter[12].

- **Section 7B** defines processes of conferment of rights on Overseas Citizen of India Cardholders. This section contains three (3) subsections. This entire section has been inserted by Act 6 of 2004 Sec. 7 and came into effect on December 3, 2004.
    - ❖ Subsection (1) spells out that, irrespective of all the laws in effect, Overseas Citizens of India Cardholders will be entitled to rights other than the rights mentioned in subsection (2). Rights of Overseas Citizens of India Cardholders will, from time to time, be defined by the Central Government by notification in the Official

---

[12]Government of India, 1955. *The Citizenship Act, 1955.* [Online] Available at:https://indiacode.nic.in/bitstream/123456789/4210/1/Citizenship_Act_1955.pdf [Accessed 12 March 2020]

- ❖ Subsection (2) consists of nine clauses [(a) through (i)]. It pronounces that an overseas citizen of India shall **not** be entitled to following rights conferred to a citizen of India:
  - Right to equal opportunity in matters of public sector employment under Article 16 of the Constitution of India (Sec. 7B(2)(a)]
  - Right to be elected as President under Article 58 of the Constitution of India (Sec. 7B(2)(b)]
  - Right to be elected as Vice-president under Article 66 of the Constitution of India (Sec. 7B(2)(c)]
  - Right to be appointed as judge of the Supreme Court under Article 124 of the Constitution of India (Sec. 7B(2)(d)]
  - Right to be appointed as judge of a High Court under Article 217 of the Constitution of India (Sec. 7B(2)(e)]
  - Right to register as a voter under section 16 of the Representation of People Act, 1950 (Sec. 7B(2)(f)]
  - Right to be eligible for being a member of the House of People (Loksabha) or Council of State (Rajyasabha) under sections 3 and 4 respectively of the Representation of People Act, 1951 (Sec. 7B(2)(g)]
  - Right to be eligible for being a member of the Legislative Assembly (Vidhansabha) or Legislative Council (Vidhan Parishad) of a State under sections 5, 5A and 6 respectively of the Representation of People Act, 1951 (Sec. 7B(2)(h)]
  - Right to be employed to public service and posts for the Union or any of the States unless such appointment is specified by the Central Government by special order (Sec. 7B(2)(i)]

Therefore, no Overseas Citizenship Cardholder of India can become Prime Minister of India.

- ❖ Section (3) utters that every notification conferring rights to the Overseas Citizens of India Cardholder must be presented before each House of Parliament.

Observation:

The above section brings the executive branch of the Government under control of the Legislative branch in matters of decisions made in the matters of the Overseas Citizen of India Cardholder.

- **Section 7C** pronounces the conditions of renunciation of Overseas Citizen of India Cardholder status. In other words, these are the conditions of renunciation of the Card that registers a person as Overseas Citizen of India Cardholder. This section, too, was first inserted by Act 6 of 2004 Sec. 7 and came in effect on December 3, 2004, for Overseas Citizens of India. Later, by CAA, 2015 the words, "Overseas Citizens of India" were substituted by "Overseas Citizen of India Cardholder" It consists of two subsections.

    - ❖ A person of full age and capacity ceases to be an Overseas Citizen of India Cardholder if s/he declares renouncing Overseas Citizenship of India Card in prescribed form and the Central Government registers such declaration with immediate effect of registration [Section 7C(1)].
    - ❖ If a person ceases to be Overseas Citizen of India Cardholder under subsection (1) of the current section in discussion, then -
        i. Spouse of foreign origin of that person who obtained Overseas Citizen of India Card under clause (d) of subsection (1) of Section 7A -
        ii. Every minor child of person who has renounced Overseas citizenship of India Card under Section 7C(1)

        - ceases to be Overseas Citizen of India Cardholder[13].

---

[13]Government of India, 1955. *The Citizenship (Amendment) Act, 2015.*

- **Section 7D** was inserted by Act 6 of 2004 Sec. 7 and came in effect on December 3, 2004[14]. This section articulates the cancellation of Overseas Citizenship of India. Under different conditions the Central Government may cancel registration of Overseas Citizenship of India under Sec. 7A (1). These conditions are enlisted under six [(a) through (f)] clauses. These are as follows:

  ❖ Overseas citizenship of India Cardholder was obtained by means of fraud, false representation and concealment of any material fact. [Section 7D (a)]
  ❖ Manifestation of disaffection towards the Constitution of India by Overseas Citizen of India Cardholder [Section 7D (b)]
  ❖ Trading or communicating unlawfully with enemy of India when India is engaged in a war and/or conducting business or commercial activity that assists enemy of India when India is in a war by Overseas Citizenship of India Cardholder [Section 7D (c)]
  ❖ Being sentenced to imprisonment with a term of minimum two years, within five years under registration as Overseas Citizenship of India Cardholder under Sec. 7A (1) [Section 7D (d)]

  Observation:

  Section 7D (d) is ambiguous in matters of the country of imprisonment. It did not spell out if the country of imprisonment of the Overseas Citizenship of India Cardholder is India or the country of citizenship of

---

[Online] Available at: https://indiancitizenshiponline.nic.in/UserGuide/E-gazette.pdf accessed on April 27, 2020.

[14]Government of India, 1955. *The Citizenship Act, 1955.* [Online] Available at:https://indiacode.nic.in/bitstream/123456789/4210/1/Citizenship_Act_1955.pdf [Accessed 16, 17 March 2020]

Overseas Citizenship of India Cardholder or any one of the two.

CAA, 2019 has inserted a clause to this section.
- Clause (da) states another condition of cancellation of Overseas Citizenship of India. That condition is violation of any of the provisions of the Citizenship Act, 1955, as amended or violation of any law in force specified by the Central Government as published on its official gazette from time to time by Overseas Citizen of India Cardholders.
- ❖ If required in the interest of -
  1. sovereignty and integrity of India
  2. security of India
  3. friendly relations of India with any foreign country
  4. the general public
  [Section 7D (e)]
- ❖ If marriage of an Overseas Citizen of India Cardholder of foreign origin who obtained Overseas Citizen of India Card due to marriage to a citizen of India or another Overseas Citizen of India Cardholder under Sec 7A (1) (b) –

1. Has been dissolved by a competent court of law or by other ways.
   Or
2. Has not been dissolved but while in the marriage the person has married someone else again.

   This clause was amended by the Citizenship (Amendment) Act, 2015.

CAA, 2019 has amended this clause further with a disclaimer (proviso). By this disclaimer, every Overseas Citizen of India Cardholder must be given an opportunity to be heard when their Overseas Citizen of India status is about to be cancelled.

Sections 8 through 10 define how citizenship of India is revoked. Section 8 defines voluntary renunciation of citizenship of India. Section 9 provides for termination of

Indian Citizenship. Section 10 causes deprivation of Indian citizenship under various conditions defined under law. These are detailed through the following paragraphs.

- **Section 8** comprises two subsections. These subsections have gone through four different insertions and deletions during amendments of 1992 and 2004. These amendments will be discussed in detail in the relevant subsections.
  - ❖ A person of full age and capacity can willingly submit in prescribed manner to appropriate authority a declaration renouncing citizenship of India. The appropriate authority registers such declarations and from the date of registration the person ceases to be an Indian Citizen. [Subsection (1) of Section 8 of the Citizenship Act, 1955 as amended]. Earlier, this subsection used to describe the person as someone, "who is also a citizen or national of another country". This description within quotation marks was removed by Sec. 8 of Act 6 of 2004 with effect from December 3, 2004. Registration of declaration of renunciation of citizenship remains withheld pending a war in which India is engaged unless the Central Government directs something else.
  - ❖ Every Minor child of a person who have renounced Indian citizenship, will cease to be Indian citizen unless within one year from attaining full age such child/ children make a declaration in prescribed form and manner and declares her/his wish to resume to be Indian citizen and, thus, becomes Indian Citizen [Subsection (2) of Section 8 of the Citizenship Act, 1955 as amended]. Previously, this subsection used to consider only "male person". The phrase within quotations was substituted by "person" by Sec. 3 of Act 39 of 1992 with effect from December 10, 1992. The conditions for resuming Indian citizenship by a person who used to be a minor child of a person who renounced Indian citizenship has included

requirement of declaration in prescribed form and manner by Sec. 8 of Act 6 of 2004 remaining in effect since December 3, 2004.
- ❖ Subsection 3 was deleted (omitted) by Sec. 8 of Act 6 of 2004[15].

This whole subsection used to deny right to residence to persons who renounced citizenship of India, on the basis of their domicile. (A.H. Magermans vs S.K. Ghosh, 1962).

- **Section 9** lays the conditions of **termination of citizenship**. This section has two subsections.

  ❖ Subsection (1) spells that any Indian citizen if voluntarily acquires citizenship of any other country by naturalization, registration or otherwise while the Citizenship Act, 1955 is in effect or in between January 26, 1950, the day the Constitution of India came into effect, and the date of commencement of the Citizenship Act, 1955, shall cease to be citizen of India on and from the day of acquiring citizenship of another country. This section does not apply to those Indian citizens who have acquired citizenship of another country during a war if India is engaged in that war. However, the Central Government can direct exceptions about Indian citizens acquiring citizenship of another country during war. *This subsection has never been amended since inception of the act in 1955.*

  ❖ Subsection (2) states that, if required, the authorities must determine by prescribed manner and with regards to rules of evidence whether, when or how any citizen of India has acquired citizenship of another country. This subsection has experienced a substitution in 2004. Erstwhile used word "person" has been substituted by "citizen of India" by Sec. 9 of Act 6 of 2004, effective since December 3, 2004, to describe whose citizenship is in question[16].

---

[15]Government of India, 1955. *The Citizenship Act, 1955.* [Online] Available at:https://indiacode.nic.in/bitstream/123456789/4210/1/Citizenship_Act_1955.pdf [Accessed 16, 17 March 2020]

The Subsection (1) of the current section in discussion has never been amended.
- **Section 10** is constituted of six subsections. These are about **deprivation of citizenship**. *This entire section has never been amended since inception of the act in 1955.*
  - ❖ Subsection (1) states that the Central Government can deprive a person of citizenship of India by order if aforementioned person has been acquired citizenship of India -
    1. By naturalization
    2. By virtue, only, of clause (c) of Article 5 of the Constitution, i.e. because of ordinary residency in territory of India for at least five years immediately preceding commencement of the Constitution on January 26, 1950.
    3. By registration otherwise than under clause (b) (ii) of Article 6 of the Constitution, i.e., migrated from Pakistan to India on or after July 19, 1948, and registered to be Indian citizen by an officer of the Government of Dominion of India.
    4. By clause (a) of subsection (1) of section 5 of the Citizenship Act, 1955, as amended up to date, i.e., because of being a person of Indian origin and because of residing ordinarily in India for seven years before making application for registration.
  - ❖ Subsection (2) contains five clauses. These clauses lay out the conditions under which the Central Government can deprive a citizen of Indian citizenship by order. Thus, deprivation of citizenship of India can occur if –

---

[16]Government of India, 1955. *The Citizenship Act, 1955.* [Online] Available at:https://indiacode.nic.in/bitstream/123456789/4210/1/Citizenship_Act_1955.pdf [Accessed 18 March 2020]

1. The registration or certificate of naturalization has been acquired by means of fraud, false representation or concealment of any material fact [clause (a)]
2. It is established by law that the citizen has shown disloyalty towards the Constitution of India or has shown himself disaffected towards the Constitution of India [clause (b)]
3. During war, in which India may be engaged, the citizen unlawfully traded or communicated with the enemy and done business which helped enemy in the war [clause (c)]
4. Within five years after registration or naturalization, the citizen has been sentenced in any country with imprisonment of two years or more [clause (d)]
    - A citizen resides ordinarily for a continuous period of at least seven years outside India if –
    i. Is not a student at an educational institution outside India
    ii. Is not serving any Government in India
    iii. Is not serving an international organization where India is a member
    iv. Does not registers herself/himself annually in prescribed manner at an Indian consulate for retaining her Indian citizenship

    The above constraints constitute clause (e)[17].

  ❖ Subsection (3) restricts the Central Government from depriving anyone of Indian citizenship unless the Central Government determines to its satisfaction that Indian citizenship of a person is against public good.
  ❖ Subsection (4) states the boundaries of power exercised by the Central Government for depriving anyone of Indian citizenship. The Central

---

[17] Government of India, 1955. *The Citizenship Act, 1955.* [Online] Available at: https://indiacode.nic.in/bitstream/123456789/4210/1/Citizenship_Act_1955.pdf [Accessed 19 March 2020]

Government requires to serve written notice citing grounds of revocation of citizenship to the person whose citizenships are about to be revoked. These grounds should abide by the conditions enumerated in subsection (2), except the condition of residency outside India as elaborated in clause (e) of the aforesaid subsection. Aforementioned persons have rights to apply in prescribed manner for referring her case to the committee of inquiry within the gambit of this section, viz., section 10.

❖ Subsection (5) lays out the norms of constituting a committee of inquiry with respect to appeals submitted through prescribed manners by a person whose citizenship is about to be revoked by orders of the Central Government. Such a committee must be chaired by a person who has a minimum ten years' experience in judicial office. Two more members should be in this committee. These members are appointed by the Central Government.

❖ Subsection (6) is about procedures of the committee mentioned in the previous subsection. The committee holds the inquiry on pertinent references in prescribed manner. Then it should submit its report to the Central Government. The Central Government takes guidance from this report for making an order under Section 10 in discussion[18].

The following two sections were repealed.

- **Sections 11 and 12 were repealed** by CAA, 2003 and 2004.[19] It was about commonwealth citizenship.

---

[18]Government of India, 1955. *The Citizenship Act, 1955.* [Online] Available at:https://indiacode.nic.in/bitstream/123456789/4210/1/Citizenship_Act_1955.pdf [Accessed 19 March 2020]

[19]Government of India, 1955. *The Citizenship Act, 1955.* [Online] Available at:https://indiacode.nic.in/bitstream/123456789/4210/1/Citizenship_Act_1955.pdf,[Accessed on March , 2020]

Commonwealth countries were listed in the First Schedule. By virtue of citizenship of any one of these countries, people used to become Commonwealth citizens of all the countries listed in the First Schedule (s.11). The Central Government by its order published in the official gazette used to confer certain citizen rights to the Commonwealth Citizens. Along with Sections 11 and 12, the First Schedule was repealed by the Citizenship (Amendment) Act, 2003 (6 of 2004), s. 16 with effect from December 3, 2004.

The First Schedule till being repealed comprised eleven Commonwealth countries and the Republic of Ireland. Eleven Commonwealth countries were:

1. United Kingdom
2. Canada
3. Commonwealth of Australia
4. New Zealand
5. Union of South Africa
6. Pakistan
7. Ceylon
8. Federation of Rhodesia and Nyasaland
9. Ghana
10. Federation of Malaya
11. Singapore

The First Schedule had an explanation that the United Kingdom constituted of Great Britain, Northern Ireland, Channel Islands and all the colonies. It has also explained that the Commonwealth of Australia constituted of Papua and the territory of Norfolk Island.

Observation:

At the time, viz., 2003/ 2004, Sections 11 and 12 were repealed along with the First Schedule, there occurred several changes in the global political boundaries. The Federation of Malaya has been an independent nation called Malaysia since 1963. In the same year, Northern Rhodesia and Nyasaland became independent of British Rule and emerged respectively as Zambia and Malawi. In 1965, Southern Rhodesia emerged as the Independent Nation of Rhodesia. Since 1972 Ceylon, independent since 1948, chose to be identified as Sri Lanka. The previous year Bangladesh was carved out of Pakistan. A decade prior to that, the Union of South Africa became the independent Republic of South Africa. After several political changes Papua became independent State of Papua and New Guinea in 1975. By the other amendments of 2003/2004 the Citizenship Act, 1955 appeared strict against migration from Pakistan and Bangladesh and provided for prevention of migration from these two countries other than by naturalization under Section 6. Therefore, without repealing Sections 11,12 and the First Schedule on the commonwealth citizenship, the entire act would have appeared contradictory. This issue was first addressed by introducing persons of Indian origin and concept of Overseas Citizens of India and the Third Schedule and, subsequently, by amendments of 2005, repealing the Third Schedule. In the recent past, the amendments of 2019, has further widened the scope of citizenship for migrants from Pakistan and Bangladesh along with migrants from Afghanistan.

- **Section 13** explains the issue of certificate of citizenship to persons if their eligibility of being Indian citizen is doubtful. In cases of doubt if a person is an Indian citizen, the Central Government can issue a **certificate of citizenship**[20]. There exist following conditions to the certificate of citizenship -
1. The person is considered to be Indian citizen on and from the date mentioned in the certificate of citizenship.

---

[20]Government of India, 1955. *The Citizenship Act, 1955.* [Online] Available at:https://indiacode.nic.in/bitstream/123456789/4210/1/Citizenship_Act_1 955.pdf [Accessed 21 March 2020]

2. Without considerable evidence, it is never accepted that the person certified for her Indian citizenship was a citizen of India prior to the date mentioned in the certificate of citizenship.
3. The certificate of citizenship holds good unless it is proved that the person obtained aforesaid certificate by means of -
    i. fraud,
    ii. false representation or
    iii. concealment of any material fact.

This is also an original section of the Citizenship Act, 1955 which has never been amended since its inception.

- **Section 14** has two subsections. They are as follows:
    o Subsection (1) gives the Central Government discretion in matters of disposal of applications for obtaining Indian citizenship -
        ❖ by registration, under provisions of Sec. 5,
        ❖ by naturalization as provided by Sec. 6
        and
        ❖ overseas citizen of India status under provisions of Sec. 7A

- of the Citizenship Act, 1955. These aforementioned sections were specifically mentioned by insertion of Sec. 11 of Act 6 of 2004, i.e., CAA, 2004. It was in effect since December 3, 2004. This section empowers the Central Government to grant or refuse any application submitted under aforesaid sections where the Central Government need not justify its decision of granting or refusing an application.

    o Subsection (2) pronounces that in matters of granting or refusing any application made under provisions of aforesaid sections, the decision of the Central Government is final. Such decisions will never be questioned by any court of law. Yet, such decisions can be submitted for revision under provisions of Section 15 elaborated in due course.[21]

Observation:
Section 14 of the Act leaves no scope for challenging the decisions of the Central Government in any court of law. Thus, this section vests absolute decision making power in the executive branch of the Government.

- **Section 14 A** asserts the issue **of national identity cards**. This section has been inserted to the original act of 1955 by Sec. 12 of Act 6 of 2004. This section comprises five subsections.
    - Subsection (1) empowers the Central Government for the followings:
        i. Register citizens compulsorily
        ii. Issue National Identity card to citizens
        This subsection was a source of huge controversy almost a decade later after its insertion in the Act.
    - Subsection (2) provides for the Central Government to maintain a National Register for Indian Citizens. It also provides for establishing a National Registration Authority by the Central Government for maintaining aforesaid register.
    - Subsection (3) vests duty of National Registration Authority in the Registrar General of India on and from date of commencement of the Citizenship (Amendment) Act, 2003. National Registration Authority has been appointed under subsection (1) of section (3) of Registration of Birth and Death Act, 1969. Subsection (3) of section 14A of the Citizenship Act. 1955, as amended, designates aforesaid Registrar General of India to act as Registrar General of Citizen Registration.

---

[21]Government of India, 1955. *The Citizenship Act, 1955.* [Online] Available at:https://indiacode.nic.in/bitstream/123456789/4210/1/Citizenship_Act_1 955.pdf [Accessed 21 March 2020]

- Subsection (4) enables the Central Government for appointing officers and staff to assist the Registration General of Citizen Registration in discharging her/his functions and responsibilities.
- Subsection (5) delineates that the procedures to be followed in compulsory registration of the citizens of India are to be prescribed. Obviously, the implied authority of prescribing such procedures is the Central Government. In due course of prescribing the procedure came *the Citizenship (Registration of Citizens and Issue of National Identity Cards) Rules, 2003* under provisions of Section 18 of the Citizenship Act, 1955 as amended up to date.

Observation:

Entire section of 14A has been framed in a suggestive manner. While other sections have used definitive auxiliary verbs *shall* and *will* this section has used *may*. This suggestive nature of the section ensues huge controversy. The section provides for registering the citizens of India and issuing them National Identity Card, *compulsorily*, yet *in a recommending manner rather than in a commanding tone.*

Sections 15 and 15A respectively provided for *Revision and Review* of applications of persons aggrieved by decisions of authorities in the matters of citizenship of India.

- **Section 15** comprises two subsections.
  - Subsection (1) allows aggrieved persons to apply for revision of decision of the Central Government, or any authorities as designated under the Citizenship Act, 1955 as amended up to date, about aforementioned person's Indian citizenship. The application for revision must be made before expiry of thirty days from issuance of decision of the authority. Under special circumstances, if the Central Government is satisfied that the applicant was prevented from

applying within a limited period due to sufficient causes then the limit of thirty days can be waived.
- Subsection (2) vests the authority of final decision about application of aggrieved persons, mentioned in previous subsection, in the Central Government. However, the Central Government needs to consider the application and any report regarding the application presented by officers or authorities to which it was submitted before finalizing the decision on the application.

This section, too, vests sole decision-making power in the Central Government, the executive branch of the Government.

- **Section 15A** was amended to the Citizenship Act, 1955 by Sec.13 of Act 6 of 2004, known as CAA, 2004. It consists of two subsections.
  - Subsection (1) is read the same as Section (15)(1). In addition to that it provides for disposal of applications for review of any order passed under provisions of Section 14A of the Citizenship Act, 1955, as amended. The disposal of review should follow procedure provided by clause (ia) of Subsection (2) of Section 18, discussed herein due course.
  - Subsection (2) vests sole discretion of making orders, in response to submitted applications, in the Central Government.

Like the previous two sections, this section, too, does not allow intervention of the judiciary over the decisions made by the Central Government.

- **Section 16** provides for *delegation of power* by the Central Government of India under Sections of the Citizenship Act, 1955 as amended up to date. It elaborates that leaving provisions of Section 10 and Section 18, the Central Government can issue orders to delegate power to officers or authorities as the Central Government thinks fit under given conditions.

- **Section 17** defines *offences* against the act and probable punishment for proven offenders. This section specifically mentions that representations by false material particulars to obtain positive or negative outcomes as defined in the Citizenship Act, 1955 as amended is a punishable offence. The punishment is defined as imprisonment for maximum five years or a fine of maximum fifty thousand rupees. The maximum tenure of imprisonment has been extended from six months to five years by Sec. 14 of Act 6 of 2004. This same act has determined the amount of fine substituting erstwhile provision of an unspecified amount of fine.
- **Section 18** vests in the Central Government of India the *power to make rules* under provisions of the Citizenship Act, 1955 as amended. The section has been defined through four subsections.
  - Subsection (1) mentions that the Central Government can make rules for the purpose of the act under discussion by publishing notifications on its official gazette.
  - Subsection (2) is hugely amended, over five different amendments. It consists of fourteen clauses. It delineates the matters on which the rules can be made by the Central Government.
    - ❖ Clause (a) provides for registration of anything needed to be registered and conditions of such registrations and restrictions pertaining to registration.
    - ❖ Clause (aa) was amended by Sec. 15 of Act 6 of 2004. It provides for the forms and manners for making declaration to obtain citizenship of India by descent defined under various conditions stated through clauses and subclauses under subsection (1) of Section 4 of the Citizenship Act, 1955, as amended.

- ❖ Clause (b) specifies that rules can be made for forms to be used and registers to be maintained under the act in discussion.
- ❖ Clause (c) defines the followings:
1. the administration and taking oath of allegiance under provisions of the act in discussion,
2. the time limits and manner of taking oath of allegiance and processes of recording such events.

   These are the conditions pertaining to the oath of allegiance.
- ❖ Clause (d) enables rule making for giving notice by any person under provisions of this act.
- ❖ Clause (e) spells out rule making capacity with respect to cancellation of registration of persons and cancellation of certificate of naturalization relating to persons if they have been deprived of citizenship under this act. This clause also enables the Central Government to make rules regarding delivering certificates to respective persons.
- ❖ Clause (ee) gives way to making rules about manners and forms for making declarations and authority to which such declarations are to be submitted. Aforesaid declarations are pertaining to provisions of subclauses (a) and (b) of subsection (6) of section 6A about citizenship of persons covered by Assam Accord. This clause was amended by Sec. 3 of Act 65 of 1985.
- ❖ Clause (eea) has been inserted by CAA, 2015. It proclaims that the Central Government can also make rules regarding the conditions and manner in which a person can be registered to be Overseas citizenship of India Cardholder under Sec. 7A(1)
- ❖ Clause (eeb), too, has been amended by the Citizenship (Amendment) Act, 2015. It empowers the Central Government for making rules defining the manner of making declaration for renunciation

of Overseas citizenship of India Card under Sec. 7C(1).

CAA, 2019 has inserted clause (eei). It mentions that the Central Government can make rules on the conditions, restrictions and manner of granting certificate of registration or certificate of naturalization under Sec, 6B (1).

- ❖ Clause (f) provides for making rules for registering births and deaths of persons born and dying outside India.
- ❖ Clause (g) enables making rules for collecting levies due to applications, registrations, declarations and certificates, also due to taking oath of allegiance and for supplying certified or other copies of documents.
- ❖ Clause (h) allows for making rules for –

1. the authority for determining the question of acquisition of citizenship of another country,
2. the procedure to be followed by such authority,

   and

3. pertaining evidence for acquisition of citizenship of another country.

   The objective of this clause is investigation on acquisition of citizenship of another country.

- ❖ Clause (i) empowers to make rules regarding procedures to be followed by committees appointed under provisions of Sec. 10 about deprivation of citizenship and conferring any right, power, privilege of civil court on such committee.
- ❖ Clause (ia) has been added by amendments of 2004. It provides the ability of the Central Government to make rules regarding procedures to be followed for registering citizens of India compulsorily under subsection (5) of sec. 14A.

- ❖ Clause (j) enables the Central Government for making rules about the manner in which application of revision may be made under Sec. 15 and, also, about the procedure that the Central Government needs to follow while dealing with such applications.
- ❖ Clause (k) enables the Central Government to make rules on matters pertaining to the Citizenship Act, 1955, as amended, not mentioned hitherto.

These rules are mostly immune from approval by the legislature and the judicial review.

- o Subsection (3) determines that the breach of any rule made under this section is punishable with fine. The amount of fine is to be maximum of one thousand rupees if such breach is not made against provisions of clause (ia) Subsection (2) of current section in discussion. For breach of rules made under clause (ia) Subsection (2) of current section in discussion, i.e., a breach regarding rules on registering citizens of India compulsorily, the punishment is imprisonment of maximum term of three month or fine of maximum five thousand rupees or both. With amendment of clause (ia) of subsection (2) the punishment related to breach of rules made under provisions of this clause was amended by Sec.15 of Act 6 of 2004.
- o Subsection (4) states that all rules made under this section must be presented before each House of the Parliament, for a total period of thirty days, while the Parliament is in session. The thirty-day period may be in a single session or in two or more consecutive sessions. If both the Houses agree before expiry of aforesaid thirty-day period about modification(s) required in the rules, then the rules come in effect with recommended modification(s). If both the Houses of the Parliament agree that the rules should not be made, then the rules do not come into effect. However, modifications or annulment of rules does

not affect any action taken under the rule prior to its modification or annulment. [22]

In nutshell, this section empowers the Central Government for making rules under provisions of the whole Act.

- **Section 19** was repealed by Section 2 of *Repealing and Amending Act, 1960* (Act 58 of 1960).

Then there is the *Second schedule* laying out Oath of Allegiance. It has been spelled out as follows verbatim:

I, A/B .... do solemnly affirm (or swear) that I will bear true faith and allegiance to the Constitution of India as by law established, and I will faithfully observe the laws of India and fulfil my duties as a citizen of India.

The *third schedule* has already been discussed along with the sections of Naturalization, viz., Section 6 of the Citizenship Act (1955). Also already deleted, the Fourth Schedule has already been discussed under Section 2 and 7A through 7D.

Summary:

At inception, the Citizenship Act, 1955 comprised a total of nineteen (19) sections. Over subsequent amendments and repealing, the total number of the sections in the Act has been changed. In 1960, Section 19 was repealed. In 2004, Sections 11 and 12 were omitted. Thus, the total number of reductions stands at three (3).

There have been insertions of Sections 6A, 7A, 7B, 7C, 7C, 14A, 15A. Thus, the total number of insertions stands at seven (7). Therefore, after getting rid of three (3) sections and adding seven (7) more sections, the total number of sections, at present, in the Act stands at twenty-three (23 = 19-3+7). All twenty-three sections of the Act can be tabulated under different categories and subcategories in the following table.

---

[22]Government of India, 1955. *The Citizenship Act, 1955*. [Online] Available at:https://indiacode.nic.in/bitstream/123456789/4210/1/Citizenship_Act_1955.pdf [Accessed on March , 2020]

Table of Categories and Subcategories of Sections in the Citizenship Act, 1955, as Amended up to Date

Category	Subcategory	Sections
Short Title		1
Interpretation		2
Acquisition of Citizenship	By Birth	3
	By Descent	4
	By Registration	5
	By Naturalization	6
	By Assam Accord (Special Provision)	6A
	By Proviso of (CAA 2019) clause (b) of subsection (1) of Section 2	6B
	By incorporation of Territory	7
Overseas Citizenship	Registration	7A
	Conferment of Rights	7B
	Renunciation	7C
	Cancellation	7D
Termination of Citizenship	Renunciation	8
	Termination	9
	Deprivation	10
Supplemental	Ommitted	11, 12
	Certificate of Citizenship	13
	Disposal of Application for Acquiring Citizenship by Registration (Including Overseas Citizenship), Naturalization,	14
	Issue of National Identity Card	14A
	Revision (of Orders passed under provisions of the act)	15
	Review (of Orders passed under provisions of the act leaving those u/s 14A)	15A
	Delegation of Power	16
	Offences	17
	Power to Make Rules	18
	Repealed	19

The Citizenship (Registration of Citizens and Issue of National Identity Cards) Rules, 2003

National Register of Citizenship has been constituted by the Citizenship (Registration of Citizens and Issue of National Identity Cards) Rules, 2003. The executive authority of this rule has been bestowed on the Registrar General of Citizen Registration. The Registrar General, India, appointed under the Registration of Births and Deaths Act, 1969 (18 of 1969) has been declared to be the functional Registrar General of Citizen Registration.

The rule has specified how National Register of Citizenship (NRC) will function. There is a well defined structure of administrative divisions. Mostly, the jurisdictional divisions of revenue administration have been defined to be the executive building blocks of NRC. Following are the facts laid in the Citizenship Rules, 2003 pertaining to NRC.

1. The Citizenship Rules comprises eighteen (18) sections (rules) including short title and definitions. Many of them consists of subsections laying out complete paradigm of the rules[23].
2. The definitions will henceforth be invoked as and when necessary. These are as follows:
   I. "Act" is the Citizenship Act, 1955.
   II. "Chief Registrar of Births and Deaths" is the Chief Registrar of Births and Deaths appointed under the Registration of Births and Deaths Act, 1969 (18 of 1969)

---

[23]Government of India, 2003. *Ministry of Home Affairs/ Notifications.* [Online] Available at: https://censusindia.gov.in/2011-Act&Rules/notifications/citizenship_rules2003.pdf, [Accessed 29 April 2020].

III. "Citizen" is the Citizen of India as defined under the provisions of the Constitution of India and the Act.

IV. "Director of Citizen Registration" is the Director of Census in a State or in a Union Territory appointed by the Central Government under the provisions of the Census Act, 1948. This Director of Census is deemed to function as the Director of Citizen Registration in the State and/or the Union Territory.

V. "District Register of Indian Citizens" is the register that contains details of the Indian citizens usually residing in the district.

VI. "District Registrar of Citizen Registration" is the District Magistrate of every revenue district.

VII. "Local Register of Indian Citizens" is the register documenting the details of Indian Citizens usually residing in a village or local area or town or ward or demarcated (by the Registrar General of Citizen Registration) area within a ward or town or urban area.

VIII. "Local Registrar of Indian Citizens" is a local officer, or a revenue officer appointed by the State Government at the lowest Geographical Jurisdiction which can generally be a village, or town or ward or demarcated (by the Registrar General of Citizen Registration) area within a ward or town or urban area, functioning as a Local Registrar for the purpose of preparation of Local Register of Citizen Registration.

IX. "National Identity Card" is the identity card issued under Rule 13.

X. "National Identity Number" is a unique identity number bestowed upon every Indian Citizens by the Registrar General of Citizen Registration, India.

XI. "National Register of Indian Citizens" is the register comprising details of Indian Citizens living in India or outside India.

XII. "Population Register" is a register that contains details of the persons residing in a village or town or ward or in an area demarcated by the Registrar General of Citizen Registration within a ward in a town or urban area.

XIII. "Registrar General of Citizen Registration" is the Registrar General, India, appointed under the Registration of Births and Deaths Act, 1969 (18 of 1969) functioning as the Registrar General of Citizen Registration, India.

An insertion was made at this point of the rule by Inserted by G.S.R. 803(E). dated. 9th November, 2009 (with effect from 9/11/2009). It defined "Schedule" as a schedule appended to this rule. This was part of the amendment of 2009 of the Citizenship Rule, 2003.

XIV. "State Register of Indian Citizens" is the register comprising details of Indian citizens, usually residing in the State.

XV. "Sub-district of Taluk Registrar of Indian Citizens" is the sub-district Magistrate or Taluk Executive Magistrate of every sub-district or Taluk functioning as Sub-district or Taluk Registrar of Citizen Registration.

XVI. "Sub-district Register of Citizen Registration" is the register consisting of details of the Indian Citizens usually residing in a Taluk or of the sub-district.

These definitions are similar to the definitions stated in any act.

3. National Register of Indian Citizens (NRC):

By amendments of this rule in 2009[24], an order for constituting National Population Register was published by

---

[24] http://www.nrcassam.nic.in/images/pdf/citizenship-rules.pdf

the central Government on March 15, 2010. By this order field work for collection of data from all residents under Local Registers was performed from April 1, 2010 to September 30, 2010. The purpose of preparation of National Population Register was issuing national identity cards and preparation of National Register of Indian Citizens[25].

    I. It should be established by the Registrar General of Citizenship Registration.
    II. There are sub-parts in NRC, viz. State Register of Indian Citizens, District Register of Indian Citizens, Sub-district Register of Indian Citizens and Local Register of Indian Citizens. These registers should include details that the Central Government, under its authority, in consultation with the Registrar General of Citizen Registration, may specify.
    III. The particulars of the citizens to be recorded in NRC are –
   i. Name
   ii. Father's name
   iii. Mother's name
   iv. Sex
   v. Date of birth
   vi. Place of birth
   vii. Residential address (present and permanent)
   viii. Marital status (if ever married, name of the spouse)
   ix. Visible identification mark
   x. Date of registration of Citizen
   xi. Serial number of registrations as Citizen
   xii. National Identity Number.

---

[25] Ministry of Home Affairs (Office of Registrar General, India), Order No. S.O. 596(E), dated 15th March, 2010, published in the Gazette of India, Extra., Part H, No. 504S.3(ii). dated 16th March, 2010 p.1.

Observation:

The first eight attributes are all required in an Indian Passport and Aadhar Card.

    IV.   The central Government is bestowed upon with the authority of issuing an order for deciding a date by which Population Register shall be prepared by collecting all information relating to all persons residing within the jurisdiction of Local Registrar.

    V.   After due verification made from the Population Register, the details of the person will be contained in the Local Register of Indian Citizens.

Observation:

It appears that local information on persons always remains with the local authorities of the Register of Indian Citizens.

4. Preparation of National Register of Indian Citizens:
    I. Collection of particulars, including the citizenship status, for each family and individual, in a local area, by enumerating from house to house, has to be initiated by the Central Government for the purpose of NRC. [Sub-rule 1]
    II. Notification about period and duration of the enumeration is to be declared by the Registrar General of Citizen Registration in the official gazette. [Sub-rule 2]
    III. Verification of Population Registrar at Local level with respect to the particulars collected from every family and individual is the responsibility of the Local Registrar. However, Local Registrar can be assisted by one or more persons as specified by the Registrar General of Citizen Registration. [Sub-rule 3]

IV. Enquiry should be recommended by the Local Registrar for the individual and family with doubtful citizenship status and this individual or family must be notified about the enquiry in prescribed proforma immediately after the verification process is over. [Sub-rule 4]
V. Hearings and findings [Sub-rule 5]
   i. Hearing of the individual or family with doubtful citizenship status by the Sub-district or Taluk Registrar should be conducted before a decision of including or excluding the individual or family in question is made.
   ii. Finding should be finalized by Sub-district or Taluk Registrar within ninety (90) days of entry being made. The ninety-day period can be extended reasonably by the Sub-district or Taluk Registrar if the reason for extension is recorded in writing.

   This hearing would never occur in a court of law. This is solely an executive procedure.
VI. Draft [Sub-rule 6]
   i. Publication of the draft of the Local Register of Indian Citizens should be by Sub-district or Taluk Registrar for inviting any <u>objection</u> or <u>inclusion</u> of names and corrections of particulars collected from family or individual and proposed to be included in the final National Register of Indian Citizen
   ii. Objections against any particular entry and inclusion of name or correction in the Local Register of Indian Citizen must be done within a period of thirty (30) days from date of publication of draft of the Local Register of Indian Citizens

recording details of reasons of objection in form specified by the Registrar General of the Citizen Registration.

    iii. Subdistrict or Taluk Registrar's consideration on objections needs to be disposed summarily within ninety (90) days and, then, to submit the Local Register of Indian Citizens to District Registrar of Citizen Registration. The latter will transfer the entries of Local Register of Indian Citizens to National Register for Indian Citizens.

Every officer would consider the objections on Register prepared by its lower administrative unit within a stipulated time period from publication of the draft and, then, would submit the draft to its higher administrative unit.

VII. Appeal, Final Decision, Documentation [Sub-rule 7]

    i. Appeal by any person aggrieved by the orders of Sub-district or Taluk Registrar of Citizen Registration under Sub-rules (5) and (6) may prefer an appeal within thirty (30) days from date of such order.

    ii. Final Decision should be made by the District Registrar of Indian Citizens Registration after hearing the aggrieved person within a period of ninety (90) days from the date of appeal.

    iii. Documentation of the particulars collected from families and individuals must be entered in National Register of Indian Citizens if appeal is allowed.

Thus, pondering over the appeals delays the publication of the final draft of the register.

By the amendments of the Citizenship Rule, 2003 by G.S.R. 803(E), dated 9th November, 2009 (with effect from 9/11/2009), Rule 4A was inserted. Rule 4A spelled out **Special Provisions as to National Register of Indian Citizens in the State of Assam**. It has four statements as follows:

a. Rule 4, as laid discussed through preceding pages, would not apply to the State of Assam after commencement of Citizenship (Registration of Citizens and Issue of National Identity Cards) Amendment Rules, 2009. The date is November 9, 2009.

b. The Central Government was asked by the rule to collect specified information about residency and citizenship status of every resident in Local Areas for preparation of National Register of Indian Citizens in the State of Assam. It mentioned that the citizenship status would be based on National Register of Citizens, 1951 and the electoral rolls prior to midnight of March 24, 1971.

In the initial amendment the date of March 24, 1971 was not specified. It was read, "electoral rolls prior to the year 1971". However, the phrase was further amended with the specific date and time, i.e., March 24, 1971, by announcement made by the Gazette of India, Extra., Part II, No. 130, S.3(i), dated 23rd March, 2010. p.2.

c. The responsibility of enumerating residents' residency and citizenship status was vested in the Register General of Citizenship Registration. It was the Register General of Citizenship Registration who required to notify everyone in the State of Assam by announcing in the Official Gazette the date of commencement and date of closure of the enumeration.

d. The process of preparation of National Register of Indian Citizens in the state of Assam was laid down on the Schedule appended to the rule.

This Schedule is a set of rules but only for the State of Assam. It has its definitions rooted in the Rule 2 of the Citizenship Rules, 2003. It has two additional definitions as followings:

i. "National Register of Citizens, 1951" stands for the Register containing details of Indian Citizens residing in the State of Assam, as mentioned in the National Register of Citizens, prepared along with census data of 1951 under directives of Ministry of Home Affairs.

ii. "Electoral Rolls up to midnight of March 24, 1971" has been explained to be the electoral rolls prepared by the Election Commission of India or by the State Election Commission of the State of Assam up to midnight of March 24, 1971. Such electoral rolls supposedly contain details of voters.

This Schedule ordered the district magistrates of Assam to publish National Register of Citizens, 1951 and three of subsequent voter rolls published until the midnight of March 24, 2011. These documents were asked to be published in sufficient number. The district Magistrate was further instructed to distribute the aforementioned lists among the public in a village or municipal ward through the Local Registers of Citizen Registration. The Local Register of Citizen Registration was asked to distribute the aforesaid documents from a centrally selected public place. That place should be used for issue of forms and collection of filled up forms and issue of receipts against collection of filled up forms. The schedule made the Local Register of Citizen Registration the custodian of the records and made them display the records during office hours. The Schedule, further, asked the Local Register of Citizen Registration to verify the applications by comparing with the aforesaid documents and prepare a consolidated list including only two kinds of persons-

i. Persons listed in the electoral rolls prior to the year 1971 and in the National Register of Indian Citizens, 1951

ii. Descendants of the persons mentioned in the previous clause.

This Schedule has also specified the process of scrutiny of application submitted by individuals. The process of scrutiny is as described in the preceding paragraph. Besides, it has directed to exclude people identified as illegal immigrant and foreigners by the competent authority form the consolidated lists. It has made clear that people who –

i. entered the State of Assam in between 1966 and March 25, 1971 and registered themselves with the Foreigner Registration Regional Officer,

ii. were not declared illegal immigrants

iii. or foreigners

- by the competent authorities are eligible to be included in the consolidated list. It has also mentioned that the original inhabitants of Assam and their descendants whose Indian Citizenship has been established beyond reasonable double, would make it to the consolidated list. Whenever in doubt, the Local Register of Citizen Registration can seek advice of the District Magistrate and must intimate the matter of consultation to the person in doubt. The same Local Register of Citizen Register has instructed to verify through appropriate communications the information about residency of people outside the State of Assam or in districts other than that of application submission in Assam before March 25, 1971. This verification became a must after 2010 amendments of this Schedule. Previously, in the original schedule of 2009 the matter of verification was a matter of discretion of the Local Register[26].

Rest of the directives of the Schedule regarding –

    a. publication of consolidated list by the District Magistrate after scrutiny, verification and authentication by Local Registers at village and municipal ward levels

    b. publication of additional lists

    c. publication of supplemental lists

    d. claims and objections

    e. appeals

- were all same as rest of the original rule of 2003. The time limits of raising claims, objections and appeals on a consolidated and additional lists and Government Officials' response time window are all same as that of the original rule.

    5. Officials of the Central Government, State Governments, Local bodies are to assist the Registrar General of

---

[26] Noti. No. G.S.R. 237(E), dated 23rd March, 2010, published in the Gazette of India, Extra., Part II, 130, S.3(i), dated 23rd March, 2010. p.2

Citizen Registration for entering data on each family and every person in the National Citizen Register and in implementing provisions of the rule under discussion.

6. Initialization of National Register of Indian Citizens (NRC):
   I. the Registrar General of Citizen Registration should make notification of countrywide NRC;
   II. instead of single date it can be a period of time;
   III. every individual must get registered with local registrars within specified period of time;

   The registration of citizens begins with the local registers.

7. Head of the family and individual to act as informant:
   I. Compulsory for every citizen to assist the officials responsible for preparation of NRC under Rule 4 and get herself or himself registered under the Local Register of Indian Citizens during the initialization period.
   II. Correct details of names and number of family members and other particulars must be provided by the head of every family during the period specified for preparation of population register as specified in the sub-rule (3) of Rule 3.
   III. Individual responsibility of being registered with the Local Registrar of Citizen Registration and to provide particulars correctly lies on every citizen.
   IV. For minors, i.e., family members younger than eighteen years of age, and the persons especially able, the responsibility of providing particulars is vested in the head of the family.

   With respect to NCR, a lot of burden of registering citizens rests on the head of the family and individual.

8. Power of District Registrar, Sub-district or Taluk Registrar or Local Registrar of Citizen Registration to obtain information:

If anyone is asked by aforementioned officials to provide information about citizenship status of any individual, then compliance is compulsory.

9. Procedure for making entries in National Register of Indian Citizens:

   Procedure to be followed for -
   I. preparing National Register of Citizens,
   II. disposal of claims and objections with respect to family or individual particulars, that are proposed to be entered into aforesaid register,

   - can be specified by the Registrar General of Citizen Registration by issuing relevant orders.

10. Deletion of name and particulars from National Register of Indian Citizens:
    I. Deletion can be made by the Registrar General of Citizen Registration in matters of
       i. Death
       ii. Ceasing to be Indian Citizen under section 8 of the Citizenship of India Act, 1955 as amended, i.e., when a person declares through prescribed forms that the person would cease to be Indian citizen from a specified date and the person's minor child/ children ceases to be citizen of India along with the person.
       iii. Revocation of Indian citizenship
       iv. Incorrect particulars

       This can also be done by any official authorized by the Registrar General of Citizen Registration.

    II. Duty of the Indian Citizen to inform the cessation of her citizenship to the District Registrar of Citizenship Registration within a period of thirty days under clause (ii) of Sub-rule

(1), that is what has been discussed in previous point.

III. Nearest relative is required to be notified in the matter of deletion due to death.

The persons aggrieved with decision of deletion by authority may appeal against order of deletion within thirty days from date of issuing the order.

IV. Appeal is disposed of after the appellant is provided an opportunity to be heard.

This provision indicates that the whole process of NRC is dynamic and continuous.

11. Maintenance and updating of National Register of Indian Citizens:
    I. The Registrar General of Citizen Registration is responsible for continuous update of the National Register of Indian Citizens in electronic and some other forms on the basis of other Registers specified under the Registration of Birth and Death Act, 1969 (18 of 1969) and the Citizenship Act, 1955.
    II. Responsibility lies with the head of each family to enter death and birth in their respective families in the Local Register of Indian Citizens.
    III. Responsibility of the Chief Registrar of Births and Deaths and other officials is to assist the Registrar General of Citizenship Registration to update the NRC.

This provision, too, implies that NRC is an ever-ongoing process.

12. Modification of entries in National Register of Indian Citizens:

On receipt of applications from concerned persons for modifications of data on the National Register for Citizens, verifications are made by designated officials. Then, the Sub-district or Taluk Registrar may authorize modification of entries as requested through

applications by concerned persons. Such modifications can be made on following matters –
   I. Change of name,
   II. The name of applicant's parents if applicant's status has been altered by adoption under the relevant laws,
   III. Change of residential address,
   IV. Change of marital status,
   V. Change of sex.

This provision emanates that the rules are made by members of quite liberal society.

13. Issue of National Identity Cards:

The Registrar General of Citizen Registration or any officer authorized by the Registrar General of Citizen Registration shall issue National Identity Card to every citizen of India whose particulars, viz., Name, Father's name, Mother's name, Sex, Date of birth, Place of birth, Residential address (present and permanent), Marital status (if ever married, name of the spouse), Visible identification mark, Date of registration of Citizen, Serial number of registrations as Citizen, National Identity Number, as mentioned in sub-rule (3) of Rule 3 discussed before in this chapter, have been entered in the National Register of Indian Citizens.

14. . National Identity Cards to be Government property and responsibility of Citizens to keep them properly:

The details of this rule are as follows: -
   I. The National Identity Card shall be the property of the Central Government and the Central Government will be its sole owner.
   II. Willful destruction, alteration, transfer and use in any form for unlawful purposes of National Identity Card are prohibited.
   III. Surrender - The concerned citizen or the citizen's nearest relative must surrender the citizen's National Identity Card in events mentioned in sub-rule (1) of Rule 10, which are Death,

  Cessation to be Indian citizen, Revocation of Indian citizenship, event of providing Incorrect Particulars to the Registrar General of Citizen Registration or any other authorized officer acting on his behalf.

IV. Loss - In case of loss of National Identity Card, the citizen whose National Identity Card has been lost or the citizen's nearest relative must report the loss immediately to the nearest police station and to the concerned Authority.

By these provisions, individual citizens are custodians of public property, viz. National Identity Card.

15. Designation of National Registration Authority and officers:

 I. On and from commencement of this rule on December 10, 2003, the Registrar General of India has been designated as the Registrar General of Citizen Registration

 II. The Central Government is the authority to designate other officers as -
  i. Additional or Joint or Deputy Registrar General of Citizen Registration and such officers and staff as may be required.
  ii. A Director, and one and more Joint Directors, Deputy Directors, Assistant Director of Citizen Registration for each of the States and the Union territories along with requisite support staff,
 - to assist the Registrar General of Citizen Registration in discharging the functions and responsibilities under these rules.

 III. Rank of State Coordinator of National Registration of Citizens must not be below the rank of a Secretary in the State Government or equivalent and the State government shall notify a State Coordinator of National Registration.

Though there are defined designations for officers working for National Registration Authority, but the actual people working can hold other designations, too.
16. Supervision and Control of Registrar General of Citizen Registration over District, Sub-district or Taluk and Local Registrars of Indian Citizens:
    I. Designating Local Registrar of Citizen Registration for each lowest geographical jurisdiction namely, a village or a ward in urban areas. The purpose of designating such Local Registrar of Citizen Registration is to prepare Local Register of Indian Citizenship.
    II. Hierarchy of Supervision and Control Authority:
       The Registrar General of Citizen Registration
       (or any officer authorized by him/ her)
       District Registrar
       Sub-district or Taluk Registrar
       Local Registrar of Citizen Registration
    Supervising or controlling authority, hence, remains the Registrar General of India.
    III. Authority of examination, and issue directions regarding inclusion or exclusion of any individual or family particulars from the Population Register or Local Register of Indian Citizens lies with the Registrar General of Citizen Registration, or any officer authorized by her.
    These provisions define a clear hierarchy and chain of authority for editing NRC.
17. Penal consequences in certain cases:
    Violation of rules 5, 7, 8, 10, 11 and 14 shall be punishable with a fine which can be a maximum of one thousand rupees. Aforesaid rules are detailed for recollection as follows:
    I. Rule 5 enforces that the officials of the Central Government, State Governments, and local

	bodies are to assist the Registrar General of Citizen Registration.
II.	Rule 7 designates head of family and individual as informant compulsorily.
III.	Rule 8 empowers District Registrar, Sub-district or Taluk Registrar or Local Registrar of Citizen Registration to obtain information from any person about citizenship status of any person.
IV.	Rule 10 is about deletion of name and particulars from National Register of Indian Citizens.
V.	Rule 11 pertains to maintenance and updating of National Register of Indian Citizens.
VI.	Rule 14 ascertains National Identity Cards to be Government property and it is the responsibility of Citizens to keep them properly.

In nutshell, violation of aforementioned rules are punishable offences.

18. Guidelines for collection of particulars of individuals, verification, issue of National Identity Cards, etc:

The Registrar General of Citizen Registration, in consultation with the Central Government, may issue guidelines from time to time to the State Governments for implementation of the rules discussed herewith as and when considered necessary.

Observation:

The aforesaid rules do not specify any hierarchy of administration for entering details of the citizens residing outside India. It is only vaguely directed by Rule 5 that any employee of the Central Government if authorized by the Registrar General of Citizen Registration is bound to assist in the process of registering the citizens.

Therefore, it must be clear from the rules discussed through previous paragraphs that the Central Government has the sole authority in matters of issuing National Identity Cards and preparation of Register of Citizens. Besides, NRC is an inclusive process for inclusion of citizens pending their respective registrations since 1951. It also helps build a network of family ancestry and can be a tool for finding distant relatives.

NRC – Process Followed in Assam

National Register of Citizens is a document that contains particulars of citizens of India. Nationwide NRC was first prepared in 1951. It was citizens' particulars collected during the census of 1951. The register included all persons enumerated during aforesaid Census.

Since 1951, many Indian citizens have succumbed to natural causes. Many citizens have been included by registration and naturalization. Many citizens have immigrated to other countries and have given up their respective Indian citizenships. These changes are yet to be reflected in National Register of Citizens. Therefore, National Register of Citizens does not only exclude people but also includes people. Actually, no person has been included into it since 1951. Thus, the purpose of NRC appears more for including citizens than excluding non-citizen persons.

Assam has finalized its portion of the National Register of Citizens. It has included persons -

- In National Register of Citizens of 1951
- In any of the electoral rolls existed till midnight of March 24, 1971
- With other admissible documents issued up to midnight of March 24, 1971 proving the person's presence in Assam or any part of India on or before March 24, 1971
- and descendants of these persons. The admissible documents are detailed in this chapter through succeeding paragraphs while describing the forms of application to be included in NRC.

Compiling the National Register of Citizens (NRC) 1951 and the electoral rolls upto midnight of March 24, 1971, Assam has created *Legacy Data*. Prior to initiating submissions of people's data for their inclusion in the updated NRC, Assam has published this *Legacy Data*[27].

The *Legacy Data* was defined by the RULE 4A & SCHEDULE OF CITIZENSHIP RULES 2003 **(As amended by 1. G. S. R. 803(E), dated 9th November, 2009 (with effect from 9/11/2009.)**[28] . This rule unambiguously declared to exclude all persons identified to be foreigners by provisions of Assam Accord to be excluded from the *Legacy Data* [Rule 3(2) under Schedule supporting Rule 4A of Citizenship Rule laying out SPECIAL PROVISION AS TO MANNER OF PREPARATION OF NATIONAL REGISTER OF INDIAN CITIZEN IN STATE OF ASSAM].

Persons included in the updated National Register of Citizens (NRC) of Assam has proved one or both the followings -

1. The person's name was in relevant documents prior to March 24, 1971, which are NRC 1951 and/or in any of the electoral rolls up to midnight of March 24, 1971, in nutshell in *Legacy Data*.
2. Linkage to a person whose name was in NRC 1951 and/or in any of the electoral rolls up to midnight of March 24, 1971.

Persons who were unable to name the person included in the *Legacy Data* required to submit Application Forms for their family along with verifiable documents.

---

[27] Government of Assam, 2019 [Online] Available at: https://assam.gov.in/en/main/NRC, [Accessed on May 3, 2020]
[28] http://www.nrcassam.nic.in/images/pdf/citizenship-rules.pdf

Verifiable documents are listed through succeeding paragraphs of this chapter.

Based on the outcome of verification, persons were included or excluded from the updated NRC. Before publishing the final NRC, applicants had a chance to submit claims, objections, corrections et cetera[29].

NRC is a formulation of provisions under the Citizenship Act, 1955, as amended and the Citizenship (Registration of Citizens and Issue of National Identity Cards) Rules, 2003. Before, inviting any proof of citizenship from individual or families, the *Legacy Data* was published (Government of Assam, 2019)[30].

The documents that mentioned sufficient to be proof of citizenship of a person residing in Assam during preparation of NRC at Assam are the followings[31]:

1. Linkage to a person in NRC, 1951
2. Linkage to any person enumerated in electoral rolls (voters' list) issued upto midnight of March 24th 1971
3. Linkage to any person having land and tenancy records issued upto midnight of March 24th 1971
4. Linkage to any person having citizenship certificate issued upto midnight of March 24th 1971
5. Linkage to any person having permanent resident card (PRC) issued upto midnight of March 24th 1971
6. Linkage to any person with refugee registration certificate issued upto midnight of March 24th 1971
7. Linkage to any person with passport issued upto midnight of March 24th 1971
8. Linkage to any person with life insurance certificate issued upto midnight of March 24th 1971

---

[29]Government of Assam, 2019 [Online] Available at:http://www.nrcassam.nic.in/coc1.html; [Accessed on May 3, 2020]
[30]Government of Assam, 2019 [Online] Available at: http://www.nrcassam.nic.in/index-M.html; [Accessed on May 3, 2020]
[31]Government of Assam, 2019 [Online] Available at:http://www.nrcassam.nic.in/pdf/app/English.pdf; [Accessed on May 5, 2020]

9. Linkage to any person with Government issued licence or certificate before midnight of March 24th 1971
10. Linkage to any person with Government service or employment certificate issued before midnight of March 24th 1971
11. Linkage to any person with bank or post office accounts details obtained before midnight of March 24th 1971
12. Linkage to any person with birth certificate issued upto midnight of March 24th 1971
13. Linkage to any person with board or university educational certificate issued upto midnight of March 24th 1971
14. Linkage to any person with court records or processes issued upto midnight of March 24th 1971

Along with above documents, following documents were accepted as supporting documents:

15. Circle officer or Gram Panchayat Secretary's certificate only for married women migrating from one area to another
16. Ration Card.

Any one of the following documents were also accepted as self-attested documentary proof of relationship with persons with whom linkage was claimed:

1. Birth certificate
2. Land documents
3. Board or University certificates
4. Bank or LIC or post office documents
5. Circle officer or Gram Panchayat Secretary's certificate (only for married women migrating from one area to another)
6. Electoral Roll
7. Ration card, *and also*
8. Some specified *other* documents.

These documentary proofs needed to be submitted along with a four part form. The form consisted of personal details of each member of a family. For family size greater than six, respondents needed to add additional forms. Each side of the form allowed six members of the family to fill up their respective details.

First side of the form consisted of five numbered columns and one preceding all was for the serial number of family members. First column was split into two rows. The first row was for the name of the family member and the next was for the contact number of the same family member. Second column consisted of three split cells each asking "relationship to the head" of the family, gender and marital status respectively. Third column asked for date of birth and age as on April 1, 2015, split to two rows. Fourth column was split again to three cells each respectively documenting nationality as declared by the respondent which might or might not be accepted by the authorities, also, educational qualification of the respondents and occupational activity of the respondent. Fifth column was split into three rows and two columns. Each row asked respectively for names of father, mother and spouse if the respondent was married. The column corresponding to the rows of these names were for the serial numbers of these relations if they lived in the same household as the respondent and their respective details are filled up in the same form. All the requisite instructions for filling up the cells in the form were detailed in the bottom of the side.

Second side was about gathering domicile details of the respondent. It consists of two unnumbered columns and three numbered columns. The numbered columns were in between unnumbered columns. The unnumbered column at the beginning was for the serial number of the family member and the unnumbered column at the end was for pasting a photo of the family member. The photo was recommended to be taken with a white background. The numbering sequence of the numbered columns was continued from the previous side.

First numbered column on the second side recorded the present address of the family member and the duration of the member staying at that address. Next column asked about the family members' permanent address. The following column recorded the place of birth of the family member.

Third side consisted of four columns starting with one unnumbered column for the serial number of family members. Following three columns were numbered in continuation with the previous side. This side gathered *Legacy Data*. Only one column of the three is sufficient to be filled up. Each of the columns were further split into four rows.

First of these rows asked for the name of the person with whom linkage claimed in all three columns. Third rows of these columns asked from the relationship of the respondent with the person in the first row. Fourth rows in these columns asked for the type of the documentary evidence being shared as proof of relationship claimed with the person named in the first row.

The second row in three columns varied from "NRC 1951 Legacy Data Code", "Electoral Roll(s) upto midnight of March 24, 1971 Legacy Data Code" and documentary proof other than the previous two shared for establishing relationship with the person named in the first row of these three columns. Those documents could be any one of the followings:

    1. Land and tenancy records issued upto midnight of March $24^{th}1971$ to the person

named in the first row of the last column of the third side
2. Citizenship certificate issued upto midnight of March 24th1971 to the person named in the first row of the last column of the third side
3. Permanent resident card (PRC) issued upto midnight of March 24th1971 to the person named in the first row of the last column of the third side
4. Refugee registration certificate issued upto midnight of March 24th1971 to the person named in the first row of the last column of the third side
5. Passport issued upto midnight of March 24th1971 to the person named in the first row of the last column of the third side
6. Life insurance certificate issued upto midnight of March 24th1971 to the person named in the first row of the last column of the third side
7. Government issued licence or certificate before midnight of March 24th1971 to the person named in the first row of the last column of the third side
8. Government service or employment certificate issued before midnight of March 24th1971 to the person named in the first row of the last column of the third side
9. Bank or post office accounts details obtained before midnight of March 24th1971 to the person named in the first row of the last column of the third side
10. Birth certificate issued upto midnight of March 24th1971 to the person named in the first row of the last column of the third side
11. Board or university educational certificate issued upto midnight of March 24th1971 to

the person named in the first row of the last column of the third side

12. Court records or processes issued upto midnight of March 24th1971 to the person named in the first row of the last column of the third side

Along with above documents, following documents were accepted as supporting documents:

13. Circle officer or Gram Panchayat Secretary's certificate only for married women migrating from one area to another if their name mentioned in the first row of the last column of the third side
14. Ration Card issued to the person named in the first row of the last column of the third side.

Together, documentary evidence of second row and fourth row in any of the columns in the third side can construct the family tree of each family and can build the genealogy of communities.

Besides, the remaining side of the form documented the domiciliary details of people who stayed out of the State of Assam prior to midnight of March 24, 1971. This is for the family members living outside the state of Assam prior to midnight of March 24, 1971 who are from the state of Assam and who are deemed to be citizens of India. People who never stayed outside State of Assam upto midnight of March 24, 1971 need not fill out the only column in this remaining side of the form.

The following four pages are the images of all four parts of the application form used in preparation of NRC in Assam.

Updation of National Register of Citizens, Assam[1]

Application Form — SIDE-A

INDIVIDUAL DETAILS OF FAMILY MEMBERS

Member Serial No.	Q.1a Name of the Person in full (Start with the head of family) Q.1b Landline/Mobile No.	Q.2a Relationship to head / Q.2b Sex / Q.2c Marital Status	Q.3a Date of Birth (as declared) / Q.3b Age (as declared) (as on 1st April, 2010)	Q.4a Nationality (as declared) / Q.4b Educational Qualification / Q.4c Occupational Activity	Q.5 Name(s) of Father, Mother and Spouse (if married) in full or if they are members in this household write Sl. No. of Father, Mother and Spouse as recorded in Sl. No. column
1a / 1b		2a / 2b / 2c	3a / 3b	4a / 4b / 4c	
1a / 1b		2a / 2b / 2c	3a / 3b	4a / 4b / 4c	
1a / 1b		2a / 2b / 2c	3a / 3b	4a / 4b / 4c	
1a / 1b		2a / 2b / 2c	3a / 3b	4a / 4b / 4c	
1a / 1b		2a / 2b / 2c	3a / 3b	4a / 4b / 4c	
1a / 1b		2a / 2b / 2c	3a / 3b	4a / 4b / 4c	

Q.2a Head/Self....1, Spouse....2, Son/Daughter....3, Grandson....4, Granddaughter....5, Father/Mother....6, Grandfather/Grandmother....7, Great Grandfather....8, Great Grandmother....9, Father/Mother in Law....10, Legal Guardian....11, International Head....12, Others, please specify....13

Q.2b Male....1, Female....2, Others....3

Q.2c Never married....1, Currently married....2, Widowed....3, Separated....4, Divorced....5

Q.3a as per English Calendar (DD/MM/YYYY)

Q.4a If Indian' write 'I' else write the name of the country

Q.4b Educational Qualification of Individual Member: Illiterate....1, Literate but below primary....2, Primary....3, Middle....4, Secondary....5, Higher Secondary....6, Graduate or Higher....7, Others, please specify....8

Q.4c Occupational Activity of Individual Member: Salaried....1, Self employed....2, Business....3, Agriculture....3, Daily wage worker....4, Unemployed....5, Domestic Help/Worker....6, Others, please specify....7

[2] The first Application Form will start with the head of family as Sl. No. "1". In case of families having more than 6 (six) members additional Forms shall be used, with Sl. No. 7 onwards.

[3] Note: Nationality recorded is as declared by the Applicant. This does not confer any right to Indian Citizenship.

[1] The Updation of NRC, 1951 in Assam is carried out under the provisions of The Citizenship Act,1955 (Section 6A) and The Citizenship (Registration of Citizenship and Issue of National Identity Cards) Rules, 2003 (Rule 4A and Schedule) as amended in 2009 and 2010.

Updation of National Register of Citizens, Assam — Application Form — SIDE-B

INDIVIDUAL DETAILS OF FAMILY MEMBERS

Member Serial No.	Q.6a Present Address (If all family members have same address as that of head write 'same') Q.6b Duration of Stay (In years as on 1st April 2015)	Q.7 Permanent Address (If same as Q. 6a write 'same', otherwise write complete address)	Q.8 Place of Birth	Current Colour Photograph with white background to be pasted (not to be stapled)
	6a House/Building/Apartment No. Locality/Town Area/Post Office Village/Town — Circle — District 6b □□□□ State/Country	House/Building/Apartment No. Locality/Town Area/Post Office Village/Town — Circle — District State/Country	Village/Town District State/Country	Photo 2.5cm X 2.5cm
	6a House/Building/Apartment No. Locality/Town Area/Post Office Village/Town — Circle — District 6b □□□□ State/Country	House/Building/Apartment No. Locality/Town Area/Post Office Village/Town — Circle — District State/Country	Village/Town District State/Country	Photo 2.5cm X 2.5cm
	6a House/Building/Apartment No. Locality/Town Area/Post Office Village/Town — Circle — District 6b □□□□ State/Country	House/Building/Apartment No. Locality/Town Area/Post Office Village/Town — Circle — District State/Country	Village/Town District State/Country	Photo 2.5cm X 2.5cm
	6a House/Building/Apartment No. Locality/Town Area/Post Office Village/Town — Circle — District 6b □□□□ State/Country	House/Building/Apartment No. Locality/Town Area/Post Office Village/Town — Circle — District State/Country	Village/Town District State/Country	Photo 2.5cm X 2.5cm
	6a House/Building/Apartment No. Locality/Town Area/Post Office Village/Town — Circle — District 6b □□□□ State/Country	House/Building/Apartment No. Locality/Town Area/Post Office Village/Town — Circle — District State/Country	Village/Town District State/Country	Photo 2.5cm X 2.5cm
	6a House/Building/Apartment No. Locality/Town Area/Post Office Village/Town — Circle — District 6b □□□□ State/Country	House/Building/Apartment No. Locality/Town Area/Post Office Village/Town — Circle — District State/Country	Village/Town District State/Country	Photo 2.5cm X 2.5cm

Updation of National Register of Citizens, Assam — Application Form — SIDE-C

LEGACY DATA

Member Serial No.

Q.9 Particulars of entry in NRC, 1951 in respect of family member or his Parents / Ancestors
- Q.9a Name of person with whom linkage claimed.
- Q.9b NRC 1951 Legacy Data Code.
- Q.9c Relationship with the person
- Q.9d Sl. No. of self-attested documentary proof of relationship from List B

Q.10 Particulars of entry in any Electoral Roll(s) upto 24th March, 1971 in respect of family member or his Parents / Ancestors
- Q.10a Name of person with whom linkage claimed.
- Q.10b Electoral Roll(s) Upto 24th March, 1971 Legacy Data Code.
- Q.10c Relationship with the person
- Q.10d Sl. No. of self-attested documentary proof of relationship from List B

Q.11 Particulars of other Documents from List A in respect of family member or his Parents / Ancestors
- Q.11a Name of person with whom linkage claimed.
- Q.11b Sl Nos of eligible documents from List A (Sl. No. 3 to 16).
- Q.11c Relationship with the person
- Q.11d Sl. No. of self-attested documentary proof of relationship from List B

LIST A (Illustrative Documents)

Q.9b 1. 1951 NRC
(Following Documents should be issued only upto 24th March (Midnight), 1971 except Sl.No. 15)

Q.10b 2. Electoral Roll(s) upto 1971
Q.11b 3. Land & tenancy records
4. Citizenship Certificate
5. PRC
6. Refugee registration certificate
7. Passport
8. LIC
9. Govt issued license/ certificate
10. Govt service/employment certificate
11. Bank/Post office Accounts
12. Birth certificate
13. Board/ University Educational certificate
14. Court Records process
15. Circle officer/GP Secretary Certificate **
16. Ration Card

SUPPORTING DOCUMENTS #

Q.9d / Q.10d / Q.11d **LIST B**
1. Birth Certificate
2. Land Documents
3. Board/University Certificate
4. Bank/LIC/PO Documents
5. Circle Officer/GP Secretary Certificate **
6. Electoral Roll
7. Ration Card
8. Others (Please Specify)

* Answer to any one of Q.9 or Q.10 or Q.11 is sufficient
** Only in respect of married women migrating from one area to another
\# These documents will be admissible only if accompanied by any one of the documents from Sl. No. 1 to 14

Updation of National Register of Citizens, Assam — Application Form — SIDE-D

INDIVIDUAL DETAILS OF FAMILY MEMBERS

Member Serial No.		
Q.12a	Particular of residence in place other than the state of Assam upto 24th March (Midnight),1971	
Q.12b	Details of Document(s) submitted for establishing eligibility for inclusion in Updated NRC	

(Repeated entry blocks labeled 12a and 12b for each family member, with fields for Name, House/Street Name, Village/Town, District, State, etc.)

INSTRUCTION FOR FILLING UP OF FORM

In case of regular households the Application for inclusion in NRC shall be made by the head of the family detailing particulars of all family members. In case of institutional homes such as orphanages, old age homes, asylums etc. the responsibility of providing requisite details of the inmates shall lie with the head of the institutions.

The Application Form shall have particulars recorded for all individual members of the family. Each Form has the provision of capturing details upto 6 (six) members of the family. In case a family has more than 6 (six) members, additional Forms shall be used.

The same order of Member Serial No written on the first page, Side A, shall be followed throughout in all 4 (four) pages of the Form. The same shall be maintained in case of Additional Forms used by families having more than 6 (six) members.

Side A :
Instructions and codes for filling up Q.1a, Q.2a, Q.2b, Q.2c, Q.3a, Q.4a, Q.4b & Q.4c are given at the bottom of the page.

Side B
Individual members shall furnish location particulars related to (1) Present Address (2) Permanent address and (3) Place of birth. Addresses shall be written as per format indicated in the spaces marked in the Application Form. If the permanent address is same with the present address of individual member, then can write only "same" in the space provided for Q.7. Place of birth shall be written in full by all members. Duration of stay in the present address in years as on 1st April 2015 shall also be furnished under Q.6b.

Only recent colour photograph of the size 2.5 cm x 2.5 cm shall be accepted. The photograph should be pasted properly using good quality glue. In any case, staple or pin should not be used.

Side C
Any one of the three questions Q.9 or Q.10 or Q.11 is sufficient. The particulars entered in this page shall be supported with documentary proof enclosed with the Form. Documents in support of Q.9a & Q.9b, Q.10a & Q.10b and Q.11a & Q.11b shall be selected from List A (any one is sufficient) placed at the bottom of the page, which should be of any years upto 24th March 1971, and the documents in support of Q.9c & Q.9d, Q.10c & Q.10d and Q.11c & Q.11d shall be selected from List B (any one is sufficient) placed at the bottom of the page, and shall also be accepted if issued before or after 24th March 1971.

Side D
Q.12a and Q.12b shall be applicable to people who stayed in any place other than the state of Assam upto 24th March (Midnight), 1971. Persons who are originally inhabitants of Assam and their children and descendants who are citizens of India staying in place other than the state of Assam upto 24th March (Midnight),1971 may give their particulars here.

I declare that all the information provided in the application is true to the best of my knowledge and belief.

Sl. No. of the applicant in the Application Form: ☐

If continued to Additional Form write 'C': ☐

Total No. of Forms: ☐

Providing any false information would attract penalties under the Citizenship Act, 1955.

(For Office Use Only)

Location Particulars

District	Circle	Village/Town

Ward No.	Household No.	E.B. No.	Sub-E.B. No.

Type of Household (Tick ☑ on the applicable)
- Normal ☐
- Institutional ☐
- Houseless ☐

BARCODE

Use only Arabic numbers as indicated here | 0 1 2 3 4 5 6 7 8 9

Obviously, it would be difficult for anyone to be excluded from *Legacy Data* or failing from tracing ancestors in *Legacy Data* to prove herself to be a citizen of India, unless she is without any of the documents listed in the form. Thus, keeping ancestors' educational and financial documents seemed important. Otherwise, if anyone knows for sure that their ancestors were in India in prior to 1951and prior to midnight of March 24, 1971, that person needs to go through *Legacy Data* minutely. Because one can only be *sure* of ancestors' residence in India prior to 1951and prior to midnight of March 24, 1971, if such ancestor was a voter in India and lived their lives to the fullest even though such ancestor might not have land property, or accounts in bank or post office, or life insurance, or certificate or of board or university education, or passport. In India any living person can be a voter if attained age of eighteen (or twenty-one prior to 1989), and if not insane. One need not to own property, movable or immovable or to have institutional education for becoming a voter in India.

As mentioned in the Citizenship (Registration of Citizens and Issue of National Identity Cards) Rules, 2003, there was a form for correction of data for the incorrect entries in the published draft National Register of Citizens of Assam with respect to families and individuals[32]. The form was appended with instructions for filling up the form.

Through the following two pages the two-page form for correction of family and individual data is displayed through pictures.

---

[32]Government of Assam, 2019 [Online] Available at: http://www.nrcassam.nic.in/pdf/NRC%20Correction%20Form%20-%201%20English.pdf; [Accessed on May 6, 2020]

Updation of National Register of Citizens, Assam — CORRECTION FORM-1 — SIDE-A

All corrections are to be made as per information submitted in the original Application Form by applicant.

MEMBER DETAILS FOR WHOM CORRECTION REQUIRED

ARN: ☐☐☐☐☐☐☐☐☐☐☐☐☐☐

Member ID: ☐ *(Same ID as appeared in the original NRC Application)*

Name of Head of Family (HOF): _____

Field where correction required	Check Box	DESCRIPTION OF FIELD	
		Manner in which data published in Draft	Required Correction
Names	☐	Name of Member	Name of Member
	☐	Name of Father	Name of Father
	☐	Name of Mother	Name of Mother
	☐	Name of Spouse	Name of Spouse
Age / DOB	☐	Age ☐ Date of Birth	Age ☐ Date of Birth
Sex	☐	Male / Female / Other	Male / Female / Other
Marital Status	☐	Married / Unmarried / Widow / Widower / Separated / Divorced	Married / Unmarried / Widow / Widower / Separated / Divorced
Present Address	☐	House Building Name/No.	House Building Name/No.
	☐	Locality / Town/Village / Post Office	Locality / Town/Village / Post Office
	☐	Village/Town ☐	Village/Town ☐
	☐	District ☐	District ☐
	☐	Country ☐	Country ☐
Permanent Address	☐	House Building Name/No.	House Building Name/No.
	☐	Locality / Town/Village / Post Office	Locality / Town/Village / Post Office
	☐	Village/Town ☐	Village/Town ☐
	☐	District ☐	District ☐
	☐	Country ☐	Country ☐

Updation of National Register of Citizens, Assam — CORRECTION FORM-1 — SIDE-B

Field where correction required	Check Box	DESCRIPTION OF FIELD	
		Manner in which data published in Draft	Required Correction
Place of Birth	☐	[illegible]	[illegible]
	☐	[illegible]	[illegible]
	☐	[illegible]	[illegible]
Photo	☐	No Photo	Photo to be added as given in NRC Application Form
	☐	Photo shown against wrong member	Photo as shown of Member ID _____ to be shown against my name (the Member ID to be filled up in the blank section)
	☐	Photo not of my family member	Photo to be added as given in NRC Application Form of my family
	☐	Photo not submitted	Photo submitted here to be added. Current Color Passport size with uniform background is to be used. (size 4.5 x 3.5 cm)
Others	☐	[illegible]	

INSTRUCTIONS FOR FILLING UP CORRECTION FORM

1) Put a Tick ☑ mark in the box against the field in which correction is required.
2) Fill up only the appropriate box wherever any change is required. Other fields requiring no correction are to be left blank.
3) Head of the Family (HOF) / any other Adult Member will submit Correction Form(s) for all member of his/her ARN together at designated NSK/Online.
4) One Form is only meant for one member and as many forms will have to be submitted as the number of members for which corrections are required. Further, all forms of all members of one ARN will have to be submitted together.
5) Correction intended for any field should be mentioned under the 'Required Correction' column against the relevant field.
6) Correction in name of Member/Father/Mother/Spouse can be made in both English and Assamese/Bengali/Bodo (as appeared in Draft published) separated by comma (,).
7) Particulars in English (only of Member Name, Father's Name, Mother's Name and Spouse's Name) can be viewed by accessing the online Draft display Portal.
8) For Date of Birth, Pin Code etc. use only Arabic numbers as indicated here 0 1 2 3 4 5 6 7 8 9
9) All corrections are to be made as per information submitted in the original Application Form by applicant. Changes that might have occurred in status of applicants since 2015 such as in marital status, age, present address etc. will not be changed by way of Correction Form submission. This is to be noted that correction will be made only if there is any data entry error in digitizing the Application Form submitted in May – August 2015. In case of change in present address also, the same can only be indicated in the Correspondence Address section below, and not in the present address section of Side-A.
10) The Correction Form is to be filled using BLACK BALL POINT PEN only.

I declare that all the information provided in the application is true to the best of my knowledge and belief.

Total No. of members for whom Correction Form submitted ____

Member ID of the person submitting the Form (in any ID or appeared in the original NR Form)

Correspondence Address

The Updating of NRC, 1951 in Assam is carried out under the provisions of The Citizenship Act, 1955 and The Citizenship (Registration of Citizens and Issue of National Identity Cards) Rules, 2003 (Rule 4A and Schedule) as amended.

Hullabaloo about CAA, 2019

Following questions have been raised by many sections of the society regarding amendments of the Citizenship Act, 1955 in 2019. The answers to them are tricky. The references to prove these answers are the same as those for disproving them. The key to differentiation between establishing these answers and invalidating them lies in the arguments made using those references. Thus, in the court of law, the decisions on these questions, would depend a lot on the gift of the gab of the lawyers arguing for these answers and against them.

Is CAA, 2019 against the secular ethos of the Constitution of India?

Etymologically, secular means "not religious". But the Constitution of India and its inherent philosophy envisaged that secular means "not particularly preferential or obstructive towards one particular religion."

Elaborating on how the Constitution of India has defined "secular" the answer to the question in discussion would be sought. Moreover, scanning through the extent and/or limits of the religious freedom bestowed on the people in India by the Constitution of India, the answer to the above question is going to be searched.

Secular as Defined in the Constitution of India:

"The Question of Secularism is not one of sentiments, but one of law." (Basu, 2000) Secular objectives were inserted in the Constitution of India by 42nd Constitutional (Amendment) Act,1976 like the inclusion of "socialist" ideals.

"Secular", being a very elastic term, was not defined in the Constitutional (Amendment) Act, 1976. The founding fathers spelled India neither to be secular nor to be socialist. But secularism was stated to be part of the basic structure of the Constitution, as pronounced by the Supreme Court, through the promise the Constitution made in the Preamble, of Justice, Liberty, Equality and Fraternity, and as enshrined in Articles 14, 15, 16 and in Article 25 through Article 28 of Part IV of the Constitution, defining fundamental rights of Indian Citizens. Accommodation and Tolerance are the ideals of Indian secularism. (1994 AIR 1918, 1994 SCC (3) 1)

As we go through the details of the aforementioned Articles of the Constitution of India, we could see the whole paradigm of definition of secular in the Constitution.

Religious Freedom and Its limits in the Constitution of India

Religious freedom in the Constitution of India has been bestowed not only on the citizens of India but also upon any person residing in India (Article 25, the Constitution of India). The inherent condition of any person practicing, professing and propagating their faith freely is that such professing, practicing and propagating of faith and religion cannot disturb public order, morality and health. Otherwise, all persons are equally entitled to profess, practice and propagate their religious faith. Yet that does not restrict wearing and carrying *Kirpan* by the persons practicing Sikh religion. Instead, wearing and carrying *Kirpan* by the persons practicing Sikh religion has been construed in the profession of Sikh religion.

The same article empowers the State, including both the Central and State Governments, for making laws that can restrict economic, financial, political and other secular (meaning non-religious, in etymological sense) activities associated with religious activities. Also, Article 25, bestows law making power on the State for reforming, providing social welfare and opening up certain Hindu religious institutions of public nature for all classes and sections of Hindus. Further, the article in discussion has elaborated the definition of classes and sections of Hindu by including persons professing Sikh, Jain and Buddhist religions and has done so in matters of religious institutions of Hindus. **Thus, much before CAA, 2019, Hindu, Jain, Sikh and Buddhists were classified together.** Such classification is not new. This reference of classification will come in handy while discussing the next question about equality.

Article 26 of the Constitution of India equally empowers all religious denominations and their sections to acquire and to manage movable and immovable properties, to establish institutions both for religious and charitable purposes and to manage their own affairs in matters of religion. There were two conditions. All their affairs, institutions and property acquisition, must abide by the laws of the land and none of these should affect public order, morality and health.

Article 27 of the Constitution of India prohibits the State (the governments – Central, State, Municipal, Panchayat) from imposing taxes on any person, who may or may not be citizen of India, proceeds from which (tax) could be utilized in promoting and maintaining any particular religion or religious denomination. Thus, any person residing in India while practicing their own religion may never need to pay taxes to any government in India for their religious faith. Also, the governments in India can never prefer any religion or support any religion and can never tax people for supporting their preferential treatments towards any religion. Thus, the Constitution has enshrined the ideals of secularism much before including it overtly in the preamble.

Article 28 comprises seemingly contradictory clauses. In the first clause, it prohibits all educational institutions funded by the State (the governments – Central, State, Municipal, Panchayat) from providing any religious instruction. The following clause elaborates that an institution if *administered by the State* but *established by a trust or some other kind of endowment* that had imposed a condition on the institution of following some religious instruction, then such educational institutions can provide religious instruction. The final clause liberates persons attending educational institutions funded by or recognized by the State from attending religious instructions. Such persons must not be minors because the guardian of minor persons can give consent for attendance of the persons at religious worship or at religious instruction in the premises of the educational institution the person is attending.

Thus, religious freedom is personal. It is not limited to citizens. It extends to everyone within the territory of India. The governments in India neither propagate nor prohibit professing, practicing and propagating any religion or any religious denominations by individuals or groups of individuals. But governments of India can prohibit professing, practicing and propagating any religion or any religious denominations by individuals or group of individuals if such actions of individuals or group of individuals affect public order, morality and health ominously. The governments in India are not against acquisition and establishment of movable and immovable properties by religious groups unless they abide by all other laws of land. Governments in India cannot tax one individual of any religion for the prosperity of other religious groups. Religion in educational institutions is not encouraged and supports persons to seek freedom from attending religious sessions in an educational institution. Thus, the Constitution of India does not prohibit institutions from engaging in religious instructions, yet it empowers individuals attending such institutions to choose not to attend religious instructions. Thus, it preserves religious freedom of organizations and individuals together. Also, it prevents religious bigotry at both institutional / organizational periphery as well as by individual.

Within this paradigm of religious freedom, whether CAA 2019 has violated the role of the Central Government by preferring a few religions can only be judged by the learned judges of the Supreme Court. Constitutionally, the Supreme Court is the only authority in the matter of deciding if a government action or law made by the elected lawmakers is unconstitutional [Arts. 131 and 131A, Chapter IV of the Constitution of India].

However there exist several documents published by the United Nations and United States Government that contain information on religious persecution in Pakistan, Bangladesh and Afghanistan. Also, there are scholarly articles narrating religious persecution of minorities in the aforementioned countries.

Md. Rajib Hasnat Shakil noted that the state machinery worked in systematic persecution of religious minorities in Bangladesh.[33] In his article he mentioned that Hindus, Buddhists, Christians were subjected to violence by majority Muslims time and again. This article has categorized the types of persecution religious minorities went through since 2002. Most of the incidents involve destruction of properties owned by the minorities, eviction of minorities from their properties, extortion and rape of women. It has also noted forceful conversion of minorities to Islam as an act of religious persecution. This article mentioned that many Hindus fled Bangladesh since 2001 to survive against religious persecution.

---

[33]Shakil, Md. Rajib Hasnat, Systematic Persecution of Religious Minorities: Bangladesh Perspective, IOSR Journal of Humanities and Social Sciences, Volume 7, Issue 3 (Jan- Feb 2013), pp – 09-17, e-ISSN: 2279-0837, p-ISSN: 2279-0845, [Online] www.losrjournal.com, Available at: http://www.iosrjournals.org/iosr-jhss/papers/Vol7-issue3/B0730917.pdf [Accessed on: May 18, 2021]

Bangladesh 2018 International Religious Freedom Report by the United States Government described various laws of Bangladesh that discriminates minority Hindus, Buddhists and Christians from majority Muslims[34]. It has documented how authorities appeared involved in persecution of religious minorities like Santhal Christians and Hindus. Often such incidents are attributed to ineffective judicial and land registry systems. Besides, this report comprising several observations of different incidents, has reiterated observations of the article by Md. Rajib Hasnat Shakil.

Unrepresented Nations and Peoples Organization (UNPO) organized an event in the Washington DC, United States on July 17, 2019 seeking intervention on Pakistan under International Religious Freedom Act[35] by the Government of the United States. They mentioned how religious minorities like Sikhs, Hindus and Christians were being subjected to systematic discrimination and attacks by extremist groups in Pakistan. Another 2014 document by the United Nations has noted how policies of the Pakistan Government encouraged in persecution of the religious minorities[36].

In Afghanistan, Hindus, Sikhs, Christians and Buddhists face religious persecution[37], too. In some areas,

---

[34]United States Department of State, 2018 [Online] Available at: https://www.state.gov/wp-content/uploads/2019/05/BANGLADESH-2018-INTERNATIONAL-RELIGIOUS-FREEDOM-REPORT.pdf [Accessed on May 18, 2021]

[35]Unrepresented Nations and Peoples Organization, 2019 [Online] Available at: https://unpo.org/article/21577 [Accessed on May 18, 2021]

[36]United Nations, 2014, [Online] Available at: https://news.un.org/en/story/2014/06/469742-un-rights-experts-call-urgent-measures-protect-pakistans-religious-minorities [Accessed on May 18, 2021]

[37]United States Department of State, 2019 [Online] Available at: https://www.state.gov/wp-content/uploads/2019/01/Afghanistan-2.pdf [Accessed on May 18, 2021]

Hindus and Sikhs avoid resolving legal disputes through the courts fearing retaliation under blasphemy laws. Instead, they resort to dispute resolution through local community councils. Almost all women, to avoid harassment by the local religious leaders, wear one or the other form of head cover, even though their respective religions do not need them to wear one. Sikhs and Hindus used to be attacked for practicing their traditional rites of worship. The most blatant attacks were on Christians and Buddhists for their respective traditions of worship. Besides, lack of employment opportunities and other forms of discriminations forces Hindus and Sikhs to emigrate from Afghanistan. Such discrimination includes resistance to cremate their dead.

In this climate of religious atrocities, people mostly fled from Bangladesh, Pakistan and Afghanistan to India. People fled from these countries and religious persecution thereof to live in India are protected by the Constitution of India [Article 25]. Because Article 25 of the Constitution of India guarantees religious freedom to all, even the non-citizens living within the territory of India.

Is CAA, 2019 against the ideal of Equality enshrined in the Constitution of India?

The ideal of equality has been enshrined in the Article 14 of the Constitution of India. The article forces the State (the governments – Central, State, Municipal and Panchayats) to treat all persons equally within the territory of India with respect to law and protection of the laws.

However, different lawyers have argued that CAA 2019 was against the ideal of equality enshrined in the Constitution of India.[38] In the India Forum, Suhrith

---

[38] The India Forum, 2020. [Online] Available at: https://www.theindiaforum.in/article/why-caa-violates-constitution#:~:text=But%20if%20we%20were%20to,situated%20in%20a

Parthasarathy blatantly claimed that CAA 2019 is a brutal assault on secularism – which the Supreme Court has upheld as fundamental structure of the Constitution of India. He criticized even the amendments of 1985 that delimited entry of people from Bangladesh to Assam by a certain date, as discussed earlier in the pertinent chapter (the chapter on Citizenship Act, 1955 as amended, Section 6A) of this book. He is also critical of 2003 amendments that limited the definition of citizenship by birth to the offspring whose one parent being Indian citizen, the other is not residing in India illegally at the time of birth. This amendment, too, has been discussed in this book in the chapter of the Citizenship Act, 1955 as amended [Section 3(1) (c) (ii)]. The arguments by the author under discussion has claimed that CAA 2019 has redefined the illegal migrant by adding a religious test to the status of any person staying inside India. However, careful reading of CAA, 2019 does never speak of altering the definition of illegal migrant, which is, a person travelling to India without a valid passport and visa. The article has argued that by putting religious criteria to CAA 2019 is completely whimsical and arbitrary, which is not true. Through preceding paragraphs in this chapter, while discussing scope of religious freedom the Constitution of India enshrined, we have seen that the Constitution itself has grouped Hindus, Sikhs, Jains, Buddhists together in matters of opening certain Hindu institutions to the general public. CAA, 2019 has included Christians in its classification to the classification the Constitution has already made under the provisions of Article 25.

Some argued the opposite.[39] V Sudhish Pai has observed lack of legal reasoning on the claim that the CAA

---

n%20unlike%20manner.&text=The%20law%2C%20for%20example%2C%20segregates,from%20other%20forms%20of%20persecution.
[Accessed on May 18, 2021]
[39]New India Express, 2020. [Online] Available at:

2019 is against the secular ethos of the Constitution of India and it, thus, infringes basic structure of the Constitution of India. He argued that CAA 2019 can neither be invalidated on the ground of legislative incompetence nor on the ground of violation of Constitutional provisions. The author reasoned that while the law regarding citizenship comes under exclusive purview of the Parliament, the question of infringement of basic structure of the Constitution only arises in matters of amendments of the Constitution. In other words, the Parliament is the perfectly competent authority for making laws on citizenship and CAA 2019 cannot alter the basic structure of the Constitution of India as it is not an amendment of the Constitution. Mr. Pai has pointed out that CAA, 2019 does not take away citizenship from any Indian. He further mentioned that none of the state governments can do anything about the law, viz., CAA, 2019. However, chief ministers, being under constitutional oath, denying to obey CAA, 2019 are actually defiant to the Constitution they are bound to protect.

There are others who explained in detail why CAA 2019 never broke the promise of equality in the Article 14[40]. Mr. Saroj Chadha refuted that CAA 2019 violated Article 14 of the Constitution of India with respect to reasonable classification, arbitrariness in state action and treating people unequally without reason. The question for arbitrariness and inequality arose as CAA 2019 specified only three of the neighboring countries of India and excluded mentioning communities like Ahmadis, Shias and Hazaras as groups undergoing religious persecution. Mr. Chadha argued that the Constitution of India is applicable only to the Indian citizens. The communities mentioned

---

https://www.newindianexpress.com/opinions/2019/dec/26/why-caa-is-not-against-the-constitution-2081028.html [Accessed on May 18, 2021]
[40]The Times of India, 2020. [Online] Available at: https://timesofindia.indiatimes.com/blogs/blunt-frank/caa-article-14-of-indian-constitution/ [Accessed on May 18, 2021]

earlier were not Indian citizens, nor by any official documentation those communities aspire to be Indian Citizens. Besides, Mr. Chadha's article mentions that Article 14 of the Constitution of India empowers legislatures to create classifications of people, objects and transactions as and when necessary. The article also argued that CAA 2019 is just enough in classifying certain religious groups as persecuted minorities in the neighboring countries of India where these groups are distinguishable from dominant Muslim groups. The article further mentions that secular nation India is the logical nation of the minorities mentioned in the CAA, 2019, prior to partition of 1947. It reasoned that excluding Hazaras, Ahmadis and Shias is perfectly reasonable as these groups are different Muslim sects living in Islamic nations of Afghanistan, Pakistan and Bangladesh, and does not belong to any other religion other than Islam.

Moreover, in the amendments of 2005 to the Citizenship Act of India, while broadening the definition of Overseas Citizen of India, under Section 2, subsection (1), all countries have been included as the country of birth of a Person of Indian Origin excluding two countries. Those countries were Bangladesh and Pakistan.

Besides, in 1952 verdict over State of West Bengal versus Anwar Ali [S.C.R. 289] as well as in the Ramana v. I. A.A.I., A. 1979 [S.C.R., 1628] as the apex court observed, " ...... among equals the law should be equal and equally administered, that like should be treated alike...."[41] It can be paraphrased as, "right to equal treatment in similar circumstances both in the privileges conferred and liabilities imposed by the laws." (Basu, 2000)

---

[41] Basu, D. D., 2000. *Introduction to the Constitution of India*. 18th ed. New Delhi: Wadhawa. Pp 88.

On classification under the provisions of Article 14 of the Constitution of India, according to Late Durga Das Basu, legislators can differentiate among different groups of persons for varying need, nature, circumstances of the persons. Hence, for helping refugees and asylees fleeing religious persecution, legislature can amend the Citizenship Act by favoring some religious groups over others. Especially, in light of the religious persecution discussed under the previous question in this chapter, such classification appears totally "reasonable". Thus, the amendment of the Citizenship Act for protecting people of certain religion seemed "rational".

Yet some people may oppose such "reason", "rationale" and "rationality" for they may find them absurd and may argue that "reason", "rationale" and "rationality" are the matters of human perceptions, opinion and vested interests. The laws made in the Parliament, supposedly, reflect the perception, opinion and vested interests of the majority of the population of the country. As the perception, opinion and vested interests of the majority, and of the people, in general, shifts with passing time, the laws change with amendments and repeals. Until such a shift occurs, debates over laws and their amendments keep democratic societies alive. Above all, the Supreme Court is the authority in the matter of pronouncing the final verdict on all debates and questions raised on laws made in the Parliament.

References

A.H. Magermans vs S.K. Ghosh, 1962. *A.H. Magermans vs S.K. Ghosh on 20 November, 1962.* [Online] Available at: https://indiankanoon.org/doc/156969/ [Accessed 17 March 2020].

Basu, D. D., 2000. *Introduction to the Constitution of India.* 18th ed. New Delhi: Wadhawa.

Government of Assam, 2014 [Online] Available at: http://www.nrcassam.nic.in/pdf/app/English.pdf [Accessed 16 February 2021].

Government of Assam, 2014. *Office of the State Coordinator of National Registration (NRC) Assam.* [Online] Available at: http://www.nrcassam.nic.in/index-M.html [Accessed 16 February 2021].

Government of Assam, 2014. *Specimen Forms.* [Online] Available at: http://www.nrcassam.nic.in/coc1.html [Accessed 16 February 2021].

Government of Assam, 2019 *NRC Correction Form - 1 (English).* [Online] Available at: http://www.nrcassam.nic.in/pdf/NRC%20Correction%20Form%20-%201%20English.pdf [Accessed 16 February 2021].

Government of Assam, 2019. *National Register of Citizens (NRC).* [Online] Available at: https://assam.gov.in/en/main/NRC [Accessed 16 February 2021].

Government of India, 1950. [Online] Available at: https://legislative.gov.in/constitution-of-india [Accessed 20 March 2021].

Government of India, 1950. *The Constitution of India.* [Online] Available at:https://www.india.gov.in/sites/upload_files/npi/files/coi_part_full.pdf [Accessed 27 February 2020].

Government of India, 1955. *The Citizenship Act, 1955.* [Online] Available at: https://indiacode.nic.in/bitstream/123456789/4210/1/Citizenship_Act_1955.pdf [Accessed 5,7,9,10 March 2020].

Government of India, 2003. *Ministry of Home Affairs/ Notifications.* [Online]
Available at: https://censusindia.gov.in/2011-Act&Rules/notifications/citizenship_rules2003.pdf
[Accessed 29 April 2020].

Government of India, 2003. *MINISTRY OF HOME AFFAIRS/ Notification.* [Online]
Available at: https://censusindia.gov.in/2011-Act&Rules/notifications/citizenship_rules2003.pdf
[Accessed 29 April 2020].

Government of India, 2015. *The Citizenship (Amendement) Act, 2015.* [Online]
Available at: https://indiancitizenshiponline.nic.in/UserGuide/E-gazette.pdf
[Accessed 27 April 2020].

Government of India, 2019. *The Citizenship (Amendment) Act, 2019.* [Online]
Available at: http://egazette.nic.in/WriteReadData/2019/214646.pdf
[Accessed 27 April 2020].

MINISTRY OF HOME AFFAIRS, G. o. I., 2003. *MINISTRY OF HOME AFFAIRS.* [Online]
Available at: https://censusindia.gov.in/2011-Act&Rules/notifications/citizenship_rules2003.pdf
[Accessed 08 December 2020].

National Register of Citizens (NRC) Govt of Assam, 2019. *National Register of Citizens (NRC).* [Online]
Available at: https://assam.gov.in/en/main/NRC
[Accessed 16 March 2020].

S. R. vs Union of India, 1994. *India Kanoon.* [Online]
Available at: https://indiankanoon.org/doc/60799/
[Accessed 27 February 2020].

Shakil, M. R. H., 2013. Systematic Persecution of Religious Minorities : Bangladesh Perspective. *IOSR Journal of Humanities and Social Sciences,* 7(3), pp. 09-17.

UN News, 2014. *UN rights experts call for urgent measures to protect Pakistan's religious minorities.* [Online]
Available at: https://news.un.org/en/story/2014/06/469742-un-rights-experts-call-urgent-measures-protect-pakistans-religious-minorities
[Accessed 18 May 2021].

United States Department of State, B. o. D. H. R. a. L., 2017. *International Religious Freedom Report 2017.* [Online] Available at: https://www.state.gov/wp-content/uploads/2019/01/Afghanistan-2.pdf [Accessed 18 May 2021].

United States Department of State, B. o. D. H. R. a. L., 2018. *International Religious Freedom Report for 2018.* [Online] Available at: https://www.state.gov/wp-content/uploads/2019/05/BANGLADESH-2018-INTERNATIONAL-RELIGIOUS-FREEDOM-REPORT.pdf [Accessed 18 May 2021].

Unrepresented Nations and Peoples Organization, 2019. *Religious Persecution in Pakistan.* [Online] Available at: https://unpo.org/article/21577 [Accessed 18 May 2021].

www.ingramcontent.com/pod-product-compliance
Lightning Source LLC
Chambersburg PA
CBHW070420220526
45466CB00004B/1484